Off Grid Homestead S

Practical Steps for Sustainable Homestead Living

By Anthony Kujo

Chapter 1: Understanding Off-Grid Living

Overview of off-grid living: what it is and why people choose it.

Benefits of going off-grid: self-sufficiency, sustainability, and resilience.

Planning your off-grid lifestyle: considerations for location, climate, and resources.

Chapter 2: Essentials of Sustainable Energy

Introduction to solar, wind, and hydro power.

Evaluating your power needs and consumption patterns.

Deciding which energy sources are suitable for your location.

Chapter 3: Solar Power Systems: A Comprehensive Guide

Understanding how solar panels work and the types available.

Installing a solar power system: setup, components, and maintenance.

Tips for maximizing solar efficiency based on location and weather patterns.

Chapter 4: Wind Power for Homesteads

Basics of wind energy: how wind turbines generate power.

Choosing the right wind turbine for your property.

Installation and troubleshooting wind power systems.

Chapter 5: Setting Up a Hydro Power System

Harnessing water as an energy source: hydroelectric basics.

Site assessment for hydro power: evaluating water flow and terrain.

Building and maintaining a micro-hydro system for small-scale power needs.

Chapter 6: Planning Your Off-Grid Garden

Selecting crops for year-round growth and climate compatibility.

Designing a permaculture garden for efficiency and sustainability.

Soil health, crop rotation, and natural fertilizers.

Chapter 7: Raising Livestock for Food and Resources

Chickens, goats, and cows: choosing the right animals for your homestead.

Housing, feeding, and breeding livestock.

Utilizing animal products: eggs, milk, meat, and wool.

Chapter 8: Orchards and Perennials: Long-Term Food Solutions

Planting fruit trees and berry bushes for sustainable harvests.

Maintenance and pest control for perennial plants.

Planning and implementing crop diversity for resilience.

Chapter 9: Gathering Fresh Water: Rainwater Harvesting Systems

Designing a rainwater catchment system for homesteads.

Storing and managing rainwater for household and garden use.

Legal considerations for rainwater harvesting.

Chapter 10: Finding and Collecting Groundwater

Locating natural water sources: wells, springs, and rivers.

Constructing a well: equipment, setup, and maintenance.

Safety precautions and sanitation for groundwater use.

Chapter 11: Water Purification Techniques

Methods for purifying water: filtration, boiling, and chemical treatment.

DIY water filter construction using natural materials.

Storing purified water safely for long-term use.

Chapter 12: Selecting and Preparing Your Homestead Location

Assessing terrain, climate, and resources for building your off-grid home.

Clearing land and preparing the foundation.

Zoning laws and building permits for wilderness properties.

Chapter 13: Off-Grid Housing: Shelter Types and Materials

Choosing the right type of housing: cabins, tiny homes, earth-sheltered homes, and yurts.

Sustainable building materials: wood, earth, and natural fibers.

Insulation and weatherproofing for extreme climates.

Chapter 14: Constructing Safe Wilderness Housing

Step-by-step guide to building a basic shelter.

Techniques for securing housing against wildlife and weather.

Improving your shelter with insulation, solar panels, and water systems.

Chapter 15: Off-Grid Kitchen and Cooking Techniques

Cooking without electricity: solar ovens, wood stoves, and campfire setups.

Food preservation methods: canning, drying, fermenting, and smoking.

Setting up a pantry for long-term food storage.

Chapter 16: DIY Off-Grid Plumbing Systems

Setting up plumbing for water distribution without municipal systems.

Composting toilets and greywater systems for water recycling.

Maintaining and repairing plumbing systems off the grid.

Chapter 17: Alternative Heating and Cooling Methods

Heating options: wood stoves, propane, and passive solar heating.

Cooling systems using shade, ventilation, and earth-cooling techniques.

Maintaining indoor climate control efficiently.

Chapter 18: Foraging for Wild Edibles and Medicinal Plants

Identifying edible plants and mushrooms in different regions.

Gathering and using medicinal herbs for basic first aid.

Creating a forager's calendar for seasonal harvesting.

Chapter 19: Hunting, Fishing, and Trapping for Protein

Basic techniques for hunting small and large game.

Setting up fishing and trapping systems for food.

Safety considerations and regulations for hunting and fishing.

Chapter 20: Managing Off-Grid Safety and Emergency Preparedness

Preparing for natural disasters and unexpected events.

Self-defense strategies and wildlife management.

Building and storing an emergency survival kit.

Chapter 21: Maintaining and Upgrading Power Systems

Regular maintenance tasks for solar, wind, and hydro systems.

Upgrading equipment for increased efficiency and power output.

Troubleshooting common power system issues.

Chapter 22: Expanding Your Homestead: Structures and Outbuildings

Building barns, coops, greenhouses, and storage sheds.

Using recycled and natural materials for sustainable building.

Planning and implementing new projects on your property.

Chapter 23: Bartering, Trading, and Building a Community

Establishing connections with other homesteaders and local communities.

Skills and resources for bartering and trading.

Creating a support network for emergencies and cooperative efforts.

Chapter 24: Preparing for Long-Term Success

Setting goals for continued growth and sustainability.

Keeping records of production, energy use, and progress.

Reviewing and adapting your off-grid lifestyle for greater efficiency.

Chapter 25: The Future of Off-Grid Living

The evolving landscape of sustainable living and new technologies.

Environmental impact and ethical considerations for homesteaders.

Final tips for maintaining a successful off-grid lifestyle.

Chapter 1: Understanding Off-Grid Living

Off-grid living is an increasingly popular lifestyle choice that revolves around self-reliance and independence from centralized systems, including utilities like electricity, water, and natural gas. At its core, it's a commitment to creating a sustainable and resilient lifestyle where one meets their own energy, water, and food needs without reliance on public or private utility services. This could mean anything from harnessing solar, wind, or hydro power for electricity to collecting and purifying rainwater for drinking and growing food through permaculture or other sustainable agricultural practices.

The decision to live off the grid is as diverse as the people who pursue it. Some choose this path as a response to the rising costs and unreliability of modern utility systems, while others seek a deeper connection with nature, wanting to reduce their ecological footprint and minimize dependence on environmentally damaging infrastructure. For others, off-grid living is a personal statement—an opportunity to create a simpler, more intentional lifestyle that embraces traditional skills and sustainable practices. Whether motivated by financial freedom, environmental consciousness, or the appeal of a self-sufficient lifestyle, those who pursue off-grid living commit to a journey that is both challenging and deeply rewarding.

The Benefits of Going Off-Grid

Going off-grid comes with numerous benefits that appeal to those who prioritize self-sufficiency, sustainability, and resilience. These benefits not only contribute to personal satisfaction and independence but also align with broader ecological and economic concerns. Below are three key advantages:

Self-Sufficiency:

One of the most compelling reasons for choosing off-grid living is the pursuit of self-sufficiency. Being able to generate your own electricity, collect and purify your own water, and grow your own food reduces dependency on external systems. This independence empowers individuals and families to have more control over their lives and resources, ensuring that they are less vulnerable to disruptions like power outages, economic downturns, or supply chain failures. Self-sufficiency also fosters a sense of accomplishment, as it requires developing a variety of practical skills, from basic construction and farming to maintaining power systems and preserving food.

Sustainability:

Off-grid living often goes hand-in-hand with sustainability. By minimizing reliance on fossil fuels and adopting renewable energy sources like solar, wind, or hydro power, off-gridders can significantly reduce their carbon footprint. Growing food organically and utilizing permaculture techniques helps regenerate soil health and maintain local biodiversity, making off-grid homesteads more environmentally friendly than conventional urban or suburban lifestyles. Additionally, managing waste on-site, through composting and greywater systems, ensures that water usage is minimized and nutrient cycles are maintained, contributing to a sustainable lifestyle that reduces pollution and waste.

Resilience:

Off-grid living naturally builds resilience, both in individuals and communities. By disconnecting from centralized systems and learning to adapt to the natural rhythms of the environment, off-gridders develop a stronger connection with nature and a greater awareness of seasonal cycles and weather patterns. This knowledge makes them more capable of responding to environmental changes and emergencies. Furthermore, homesteads designed with resilient systems, such as water catchment tanks, diversified food sources, and renewable energy solutions, can function independently of societal disruptions—be it extreme weather events, economic crises, or other emergencies. This resilience not only protects off-grid individuals but also allows them to thrive in ways that are often not possible within centralized infrastructure.

Planning Your Off-Grid Lifestyle

Transitioning to an off-grid lifestyle requires careful planning. It's not just about installing solar panels or digging a well; it's about understanding the environment you live in, assessing your needs, and setting realistic goals. For beginners, this planning phase is crucial to avoid the common pitfalls and challenges that can arise when leaving the convenience of modern infrastructure behind.

Location Considerations:

The first step in planning an off-grid lifestyle is selecting an appropriate location. Factors such as climate, geography, and proximity to resources will greatly influence the feasibility of your off-grid setup. For example, areas with abundant sunlight may be ideal for solar power, while properties near rivers or streams may allow for hydro power installations. Windy regions, on the other hand, provide ample opportunities for wind turbines. Evaluating the natural environment of your chosen site is essential for determining which power systems will work best.

Additionally, legal considerations must be accounted for. Zoning laws, building permits, and water rights regulations vary by region, and understanding these rules will help you avoid conflicts with local authorities. Some areas may have restrictions on rainwater harvesting, while others might limit the types of structures you can build. Researching these factors early on will save you time, money, and legal complications later.

Climate and Environmental Adaptation:

Knowing the climate of your location is vital when planning your off-grid setup. For instance, homesteads in temperate regions may benefit from greenhouse structures to extend the growing season, while those in arid regions might need to prioritize water storage and efficient irrigation systems. Similarly, off-gridders in colder climates will need to plan for insulation, winter food stores, and reliable heating solutions like wood stoves or passive solar design. Understanding local weather patterns, seasonal changes, and potential natural disasters will help you create a resilient, adaptable homestead.

Resource Assessment:

Before embarking on an off-grid lifestyle, it's important to evaluate the availability of essential resources like water, sunlight, and wind. Each of these resources will influence your choices for power systems, food production, and water collection.

Water Sources: Water is one of the most critical elements for off-grid living, and securing a reliable and clean water source should be a top priority. Depending on the area, you may have access to groundwater (such as wells), surface water (rivers or lakes), or rainwater. Each source requires specific infrastructure for collection, storage, and purification. A location with abundant water resources provides more flexibility in terms of agriculture, livestock, and household use, making it easier to sustain an off-grid lifestyle.

Sunlight: Solar power is often the most practical and efficient source of energy for off-grid homes, especially in areas with high sun exposure year-round. Assessing the daily sunlight hours in your region and ensuring that your property has unobstructed access to sunlight for most of the day will be crucial if solar is your primary energy source.

Wind Potential: If you are considering wind power, measuring the average wind speed on your property will be necessary. Wind turbines require consistent wind speeds to operate efficiently, so understanding seasonal variations and the overall wind profile of your location will help determine if wind energy is viable.

Budgeting and Resource Allocation:

Off-grid living, while often more economical in the long run, does require an upfront investment. It's essential to plan your budget realistically, prioritizing the most critical systems first (e.g., water supply and energy generation). Beginners should start small and gradually expand their systems as they gain experience and resources. For example, a basic solar array to power essential appliances can be expanded over time as needs grow. Similarly, initial gardens and small livestock like chickens can be gradually expanded to include larger animals like goats and cows.

Allocating resources efficiently means making smart choices about which technologies and materials will provide the most benefit over time. While it might be tempting to purchase the latest energy-efficient gadgets, prioritizing infrastructure that supports food and water security, like greenhouses or water filtration systems, will have the most immediate and significant impact on your self-sufficiency.

Skill Development and Learning:

Transitioning to an off-grid lifestyle requires more than just planning and budgeting; it requires skills. Learning how to build structures, maintain renewable energy systems, manage livestock, and grow food are all essential skills for successful off-grid living. Beginners should invest time in acquiring these skills before making the leap. Taking workshops, reading relevant literature, and volunteering on other homesteads can provide valuable hands-on experience.

Building a network of other off-grid enthusiasts and experienced homesteaders can also be invaluable. Whether through online forums, local meetups, or community groups, connecting with others who have gone through the process can provide insight, advice, and support. Experienced homesteaders can offer lessons on what works and what doesn't, helping beginners avoid common mistakes.

Setting Realistic Goals:

Off-grid living is a gradual process that requires patience and persistence. It's important to set realistic goals and manage expectations. Starting small, such as by growing a simple garden or installing a rainwater collection system, allows beginners to learn without being overwhelmed. Over time, as knowledge and experience accumulate, more complex projects like renewable energy systems or animal husbandry can be integrated into the homestead plan.

Breaking down the overall goal of self-sufficiency into manageable steps—such as setting up power first, then focusing on food production, followed by water management—helps maintain focus and ensures that progress is steady. Documenting these steps and achievements also provides motivation, as it serves as a record of how far the journey has come.

Conclusion: Setting the Foundation for Success

By understanding the fundamental concepts and benefits of off-grid living, as well as carefully planning for the specific needs of your chosen location, you set the stage for a successful transition to a self-sufficient lifestyle. Off-grid living is not about achieving perfection overnight but rather developing a sustainable, resilient way of life that adapts and grows with time and experience. Whether your goal is to reduce your ecological footprint, save money, or simply reclaim independence, each step taken toward self-sufficiency brings you closer to a balanced, fulfilling lifestyle.

In the following chapters, we'll dive deeper into each aspect of off-grid living, from designing and implementing sustainable energy systems to building a secure home and growing abundant food. Remember, off-grid living is not just about survival; it's about thriving in harmony with nature and creating a lifestyle that supports long-term health, well-being, and independence.

Now that you understand the basics and have a foundation for planning your off-grid journey, we can begin exploring the practical steps to make it a reality.

With the right mindset, careful planning, and a commitment to learning, living off the grid can be a deeply rewarding experience. Embrace the challenges, stay adaptable, and always keep the ultimate goal in sight: building a life of freedom, sustainability, and resilience.

Chapter 2: Essentials of Sustainable Energy

Transitioning to off-grid living means taking control of your own energy production, which is one of the most critical components of self-sufficiency. In an off-grid lifestyle, relying on centralized power grids is not an option, so it's essential to design a reliable and sustainable energy system that suits your needs and location. There are three primary renewable energy sources to consider: solar power, wind power, and hydro power. Each has its benefits and limitations, and the choice often depends on your location, available resources, and power needs.

This chapter introduces these three energy systems, guiding you through the initial steps of evaluating your power consumption patterns and determining which sources are most viable based on your homestead's geographical and climatic conditions. By the end of this chapter, you'll have a foundational understanding of how to plan your off-grid energy system effectively.

Solar Power Systems

Solar energy is the most popular choice for off-grid homesteads due to its accessibility and versatility. By harnessing the sun's energy using photovoltaic (PV) panels, you can generate electricity for a wide range of uses, from powering household appliances to running water pumps. Here are the key factors to consider when evaluating solar power:

How Solar Panels Work:

Solar panels are made of semiconductor materials, typically silicon, that convert sunlight into electricity. When sunlight hits the panel, it excites electrons, creating an electric current. This DC (Direct Current) electricity is then converted into AC (Alternating Current) through an inverter, making it usable for most household appliances.

Types of Solar Panels:

There are three main types of solar panels: monocrystalline, polycrystalline, and thin-film. Monocrystalline panels are the most efficient and compact, making them ideal for off-grid setups where space may be limited. Polycrystalline panels are slightly less efficient but more affordable, while thin-film panels are lightweight and flexible but often require more space to generate the same amount of power.

Installation Considerations:

Solar panels need direct sunlight for maximum efficiency, so placing them in a location free from shade and facing the optimal direction (usually south in the northern hemisphere) is crucial. The tilt angle of your panels should also match your latitude to maximize sun exposure throughout the year.

Maintenance and Efficiency:

Solar panels are relatively low maintenance, but it's important to clean them periodically to remove dust, debris, or snow that may block sunlight. Monitoring systems can help you track performance and detect any issues early. Additionally, ensuring the batteries in your solar system are maintained correctly is essential for energy storage efficiency, especially for nighttime use or cloudy periods.

Wind Power Systems

Wind energy is another viable option for off-grid homesteads, especially in regions with consistent wind patterns. Wind turbines generate electricity by using wind to spin blades connected to a rotor, which drives a generator. For some off-grid setups, wind power can be a complementary system to solar, providing power during cloudy or night hours when solar energy is unavailable.

Understanding Wind Power:

Wind turbines capture the kinetic energy of the wind and convert it into mechanical energy, which is then transformed into electrical energy. The efficiency of a wind turbine depends on the average wind speed in the area and the turbine's design.

Choosing the Right Wind Turbine:

When selecting a wind turbine for your off-grid system, it's important to consider factors like rotor diameter, tower height, and rated power output. Larger turbines with longer blades can capture more wind and generate more electricity, but they also require more space and stronger wind speeds.

A wind turbine typically needs an average wind speed of at least 9-12 mph (15-19 km/h) to be effective. Therefore, it's crucial to measure wind speeds at your site using an anemometer over a period of time to determine if wind power is a feasible option.

Installation and Location:

Wind turbines should be installed in open areas, ideally on a hilltop or away from obstructions such as trees and buildings. They also need to be positioned high enough (generally 30-40 feet above surrounding obstacles) to access stronger and more consistent winds.

Maintenance Requirements:

Wind turbines require regular maintenance to ensure they operate efficiently. This includes checking for wear and tear on the blades, lubricating moving parts, and inspecting the wiring. In high-wind events, turbines may need to be shut down temporarily to prevent damage.

Hydro Power Systems

For homesteads located near rivers, streams, or other flowing water sources, hydroelectric power can be an incredibly efficient and reliable source of energy. Micro-hydro systems generate electricity by using the flow of water to turn a turbine, similar to how large-scale hydroelectric plants operate but on a much smaller scale.

Understanding Hydro Power:

A micro-hydro system uses the movement of water to turn a turbine, which is connected to a generator that produces electricity. The amount of power generated depends on two main factors: flow rate (the volume of water moving per second) and head (the vertical distance the water falls). Generally, higher flow rates and greater head heights lead to more energy production.

Site Assessment:

Before installing a hydro system, it's crucial to assess the water source on your property. This includes measuring the flow rate and head, and checking for seasonal variations in water levels. Even small creeks or streams can be used for micro-hydro systems if they provide consistent flow throughout the year.

It's also important to ensure the water rights for your property allow for hydroelectric use, as some regions have legal restrictions or require permits for altering water flow.

Components of a Micro-Hydro System:

A typical system includes an intake (which channels water to the turbine), a penstock (a pipe that directs water), and the turbine itself. The turbine is connected to a generator and may include a battery storage system for continuous power supply.

Depending on the setup, a micro-hydro system can generate power continuously, making it one of the most reliable sources of off-grid electricity—especially in locations where water flow is stable.

Maintenance and Upkeep:

Regular maintenance includes clearing debris from the intake, inspecting the turbine for damage, and ensuring the penstock remains free of blockages. Properly maintained, a micro-hydro system can provide consistent energy for many years.

Evaluating Your Power Needs and Consumption Patterns

Before committing to a particular energy source, it's crucial to evaluate your power needs accurately. Estimating energy consumption will help you determine the size and scope of your off-grid system and choose the most suitable energy sources.

Calculating Energy Consumption:

Start by listing all the appliances and systems you plan to run on your off-grid setup. This might include lighting, refrigeration, water pumps, heating systems, and other electronics. For each item, note its wattage and estimate the number of hours per day it will be used.

Multiply the wattage by the hours of use to calculate the watt-hours each appliance consumes daily. Summing up these values gives you an idea of your total daily energy usage.

Factoring in Seasonal Variations:

Consider how your energy needs might fluctuate throughout the year. For instance, heating requirements will increase during colder months, while cooling systems might run more frequently in summer. Solar energy production also varies seasonally, with longer days in summer producing more energy than shorter winter days.

Adjusting your energy calculations for these seasonal variations is critical to ensure your system can meet your needs year-round, even during peak usage periods.

Battery Storage and Backup Systems:

Most off-grid systems rely on batteries to store excess energy for times when energy production is low (e.g., nighttime for solar or windless periods). Batteries can be one of the most expensive components, so it's important to calculate your storage needs accurately based on your energy consumption patterns.

Backup systems such as generators or additional battery banks can provide added security during periods of high usage or low energy production.

Deciding Which Energy Sources are Suitable for Your Location

Once you have a clear understanding of your power needs and consumption patterns, the next step is determining which energy sources are most suitable based on your location's resources. Each renewable energy option has its ideal conditions:

Evaluating Solar Suitability:

Solar is an excellent choice for most off-grid setups, particularly in regions that receive ample sunlight year-round. Using tools like solar maps or consulting regional data can help you understand the average sunlight hours per day in your area. If your location has over 5 hours of sunlight per day on average, solar can likely be your primary energy source.

Consider whether your property offers suitable locations for panel installation, such as rooftops or open spaces free from shade.

Assessing Wind Potential:

If your location has consistent and strong winds (typically 9 mph or higher on average), wind energy may be a viable option. Areas near coastlines, plains, or hilltops often have the best wind conditions. Installing a small wind turbine can supplement solar power, especially in regions where sunlight may be less reliable during certain seasons.

Be mindful of local building codes or zoning restrictions that may affect the height or placement of wind turbines.

Evaluating Hydro Feasibility:

Hydro power is highly dependent on the availability of a flowing water source. If your property includes a stream, river, or waterfall, it's worth conducting a flow rate test and measuring the head to assess its potential for generating power. Even a small micro-hydro setup can be incredibly efficient if your location offers sufficient water flow.

However, keep in mind that hydro systems often require more significant infrastructure and maintenance, such as building water channels or installing debris filters. Additionally, environmental impact assessments or permits may be required depending on local regulations.

Combining Multiple Energy Sources:

In many cases, a hybrid approach using multiple energy sources (e.g., combining solar and wind) is the most effective strategy for ensuring consistent power. This approach allows for energy production regardless of seasonal or daily variations, providing flexibility and redundancy.

For example, wind turbines can produce power at night when solar panels are inactive, while hydro power can provide a continuous energy source if a reliable water flow is available. Battery storage systems play a crucial role in balancing these inputs and ensuring that power is available when needed.

Long-Term Considerations:

When designing your off-grid energy system, consider the long-term sustainability and scalability of your setup. Systems that can be expanded or upgraded as your needs change are preferable. Additionally, planning for backup power sources, such as a diesel generator or a larger battery bank, can provide peace of mind during unexpected events or maintenance periods.

Regularly reviewing and adjusting your system's components based on energy production and consumption data will help keep your off-grid homestead efficient and resilient.

Conclusion: Choosing the Right Energy System for Your Off-Grid Life

Designing a sustainable energy system is one of the most important steps in transitioning to an off-grid lifestyle. By evaluating your power needs, understanding the strengths and limitations of different energy sources, and choosing those best suited to your location, you can build a system that supports your self-sufficiency goals. Remember that flexibility is key—combining multiple renewable sources and building a resilient infrastructure will allow you to thrive independently of centralized power grids.

In the next chapter, we'll dive deeper into the specifics of solar power systems, exploring everything from selecting the right equipment to installation and maintenance tips that will maximize your solar efficiency.

Chapter 3: Solar Power Systems: A Comprehensive Guide

Solar power is one of the most practical and widely used energy sources for off-grid homesteaders. Harnessing the sun's energy provides a clean, renewable, and scalable option for generating electricity in almost any location with sufficient sunlight. Understanding the fundamentals of how solar panels work and choosing the right type for your needs are the first steps toward building an efficient solar power system.

Understanding How Solar Panels Work

Solar panels, also known as photovoltaic (PV) panels, are devices that convert sunlight directly into electricity. Here's a breakdown of the basic process:

The Photovoltaic Effect:

Solar panels are made up of multiple solar cells, typically composed of silicon—a semiconductor material. When sunlight (photons) hits these cells, it excites electrons within the silicon atoms, causing them to flow and generate an electric current. This phenomenon is called the photovoltaic effect.

The electricity generated by the solar cells is Direct Current (DC). To make it usable for most household appliances, it must be converted into Alternating Current (AC) using an inverter. The inverter is a critical component of any solar power system, as it transforms DC into AC, which is compatible with standard electrical systems.

Solar Panel Types:

Monocrystalline Panels: These are the most efficient type, made from a single continuous crystal structure. Monocrystalline panels are space-efficient, making them ideal for smaller rooftops or limited land areas. They perform well in both high and low light conditions, providing a consistent energy output.

Polycrystalline Panels: Composed of multiple silicon crystals, these panels are less efficient but more affordable. They have a slightly lower efficiency rate compared to monocrystalline panels, which means they take up more space to generate the same amount of power. However, for off-grid setups with ample space, they can be a cost-effective option.

Thin-Film Panels: These are made by depositing thin layers of photovoltaic material onto a substrate. While they are the least efficient of the three, they are lightweight and flexible, making them suitable for specialized installations, such as mobile units or curved surfaces.

Performance Factors:

Solar panel performance depends on factors such as temperature, sunlight exposure, and tilt angle. High temperatures can reduce the efficiency of the panels, while proper tilt and orientation ensure maximum exposure to sunlight throughout the day.

Installing a Solar Power System: Setup, Components, and Maintenance

Once you understand the basics of how solar panels work and have chosen the appropriate type for your homestead, the next step is installation. Installing a solar power system involves several components and considerations, including the layout of your panels, wiring, and power management.

System Components:

A typical off-grid solar power system includes the following components:

Solar Panels: These collect sunlight and generate DC electricity.

Charge Controller: Regulates the amount of power going into your battery bank from the solar panels, preventing overcharging and extending the lifespan of the batteries.

Battery Bank: Stores energy for use when sunlight is not available (e.g., during nighttime or cloudy periods). The size and capacity of the battery bank depend on your energy consumption patterns and the number of solar panels in your system.

Inverter: Converts DC from the battery bank into AC for powering household appliances. Inverters come in various sizes and should be selected based on the total power output of your system and the appliances you plan to run.

Mounting System: A structure that holds the solar panels in place, either on the roof or on the ground. Ground-mounted systems provide flexibility in positioning and angle but require more space and a stable base.

Installation Steps:

Site Assessment: Before installing, conduct a site assessment to determine the best location for your solar panels. Ideal sites receive direct sunlight for the majority of the day, are free from obstructions like trees or buildings, and allow for optimal panel orientation (usually south-facing in the northern hemisphere).

Mounting the Panels: Secure the mounting system on a stable surface, ensuring it's properly tilted to match your location's latitude. For roof installations, use secure and weatherproof attachments. Ground installations should be reinforced against wind and other environmental factors.

Wiring the System: Connect the panels to the charge controller, which is then wired to the battery bank. The inverter is connected to the battery bank and then wired to your homestead's electrical panel. Use high-quality, weather-resistant cables and secure all connections to prevent damage or short circuits.

Maintenance Essentials:

Regular maintenance includes cleaning the panels to remove dust, debris, or snow that may reduce efficiency. Inspect the system's wiring and connections periodically for signs of wear or damage, and test battery health and charge controller settings to ensure optimal performance.

Monitoring systems can be installed to track the energy production and consumption of your solar power system, allowing you to detect any issues early and make necessary adjustments.

Tips for Maximizing Solar Efficiency Based on Location and Weather Patterns

Maximizing solar efficiency involves strategic placement, maintenance, and an understanding of how weather and seasonal patterns affect your solar power system's performance. Here are some key tips:

Optimizing Solar Panel Orientation:

The orientation and angle of your solar panels greatly influence their efficiency. In the northern hemisphere, panels should face true south (or true north in the southern hemisphere) to capture the maximum amount of sunlight. The tilt angle should match your geographical latitude for the best year-round performance. For example, if you live at a latitude of 30 degrees, your panels should be tilted at approximately 30 degrees.

Adjustable mounting systems can allow you to change the angle seasonally—steeper angles in winter capture lower-angle sunlight, while flatter angles in summer maximize exposure when the sun is higher in the sky.

Incorporating Seasonal Adjustments:

In regions with significant seasonal variations in sunlight, adjusting the tilt angle of your panels can improve energy capture during different times of the year. For instance, in winter, when the sun is lower, a steeper angle may increase exposure, while a flatter angle works better in summer when the sun is higher.

For more advanced setups, tracking systems can be installed to automatically adjust the panel orientation throughout the day to follow the sun's path, maximizing efficiency. However, these systems require more maintenance and are generally more expensive.

Considering Weather Patterns:

Cloud cover, rain, and snow can significantly impact solar power production. In areas prone to frequent cloud cover, it's important to size your system with additional panels or larger battery storage to compensate for lower production days. Similarly, in regions that experience heavy snowfall, panels should be installed at a steep enough angle to prevent snow accumulation.

Having backup systems like a small wind turbine or a generator can supplement power during prolonged cloudy periods or storms when solar energy output is reduced.

Monitoring and System Performance Tracking:

Installing a monitoring system allows you to track the performance of your solar panels and identify any efficiency issues early. These systems provide real-time data on energy production and consumption, battery levels, and potential faults. Monitoring also helps you optimize usage patterns by aligning energy-intensive activities (like pumping water or running machinery) with peak sunlight hours for maximum efficiency.

Routine checks should include inspecting panels for physical damage, cleaning them to ensure optimal sunlight exposure, and verifying that the inverter and charge controller are functioning correctly. Monitoring battery levels and charge cycles is also important to maintain the longevity of your battery bank.

Installation Planning: Budgeting and Scalability

Budget Considerations:

Solar systems, especially off-grid ones, require an initial investment. However, long-term savings often offset these costs. When budgeting for your system, include the costs of panels, inverters, mounting hardware, batteries, and additional components like charge controllers and monitoring systems.

To manage costs, you can start small and expand the system over time. For example, you may initially install a few panels to power essential appliances and add more panels as your budget allows or as energy needs grow.

Planning for Scalability:

Design your system with future growth in mind. If you plan to expand, make sure your charge controller and inverter can handle additional panels. Proper planning also involves leaving space on your mounting system for extra panels and ensuring that your battery bank has the capacity to store increased energy output.

Battery Banks: Storing Solar Energy

An essential component of any off-grid solar system is the battery bank, which stores energy generated during the day for use at night or during periods of low sunlight. Here are the critical factors to consider when choosing and managing your battery bank:

Battery Types:

Lead-Acid Batteries: These are the most common type used in off-grid systems due to their affordability and availability. They come in two main types: flooded lead-acid (which require maintenance and regular water topping) and sealed lead-acid (which are maintenance-free but have a shorter lifespan).

Lithium-Ion Batteries: These are increasingly popular due to their longer lifespan, higher efficiency, and lower maintenance requirements compared to lead-acid batteries. However, they are more expensive upfront. For homesteaders planning long-term, lithium-ion batteries can be a wise investment due to their durability and efficiency.

Nickel-Iron (NiFe) Batteries: Although less common, these batteries are known for their robustness and longevity (some can last up to 20 years). However, they are bulkier and less efficient compared to other options.

Sizing the Battery Bank:

To determine the size of your battery bank, calculate your daily energy usage and multiply it by the number of days you want to store energy for. This is often referred to as days of autonomy.

For instance, if your daily usage is 5 kWh and you want a three-day backup, you'll need a battery bank capable of storing 15 kWh.

Additionally, it's crucial to account for depth of discharge (DoD), which indicates how much energy you can use from a battery without reducing its lifespan. For instance, lead-acid batteries typically have a DoD of 50%, meaning you should only use half of their total capacity to maintain longevity.

Maintenance Tips:

Regularly inspect battery terminals for corrosion and clean them if needed. For flooded lead-acid batteries, check electrolyte levels monthly and add distilled water as required. Monitoring the state of charge (SoC) using a meter will help you ensure that batteries remain within their optimal range, preventing overcharging or deep discharges.

Inverters and Charge Controllers: Managing Solar Power Effectively

Inverter Selection:

The inverter is a crucial component that converts DC from the battery bank into AC power for household use. When choosing an inverter, consider its capacity (measured in watts) and waveform type. Off-grid systems typically use pure sine wave inverters, which provide clean power suitable for sensitive electronics like computers and refrigerators.

Ensure the inverter capacity matches your maximum energy load. For example, if your total household consumption is 3,000 watts at peak, your inverter should have a capacity of at least 3,500-4,000 watts to handle the load comfortably.

Charge Controller Types:

Charge controllers regulate the power going into your battery bank, preventing overcharging and ensuring battery health. The two main types are Pulse Width Modulation (PWM) and Maximum Power Point Tracking (MPPT) controllers. MPPT controllers are more efficient as they adjust the voltage to maximize energy harvest, especially in varying weather conditions.

For larger systems or those located in areas with frequent weather fluctuations, an MPPT controller is recommended as it can increase efficiency by up to 30% compared to PWM controllers.

Optimizing System Performance:

Keep the inverter, charge controller, and battery bank in a well-ventilated, dry location to prevent overheating. Regularly check for software updates for monitoring systems to keep your setup operating at peak efficiency.

Balance your load by using energy-intensive appliances (e.g., washing machines, pumps) during peak sunlight hours when energy production is highest.

Scaling and Future-Proofing Your Solar System

Designing for Expansion:

As your off-grid homestead grows, your energy needs may increase. Designing a system that allows for easy expansion is crucial. Ensure your initial setup includes an inverter and charge controller that can handle additional panels and batteries without needing to replace major components.

Installing a modular racking system that can accommodate more panels is a practical approach for future scalability.

Integrating with Other Energy Systems:

Combining solar power with other energy sources like wind or hydro can increase your system's reliability and versatility. Hybrid systems are becoming more popular as they provide a more consistent energy supply. For instance, when solar output is low due to overcast skies, a wind turbine can fill the gap.

Additionally, incorporating a backup generator can offer peace of mind during prolonged periods of low solar output. Ensure that the generator is integrated with an automatic transfer switch to seamlessly switch between energy sources without manual intervention.

Future Innovations:

The solar energy field is continuously evolving, with innovations like solar roof tiles, high-efficiency panels, and better storage solutions becoming more accessible. Keeping informed about new developments can allow you to upgrade your system incrementally as technology advances, ensuring long-term efficiency and reliability.

Conclusion: Building an Efficient Solar Power System

A well-designed solar power system is a foundational element for any off-grid homestead. By understanding how solar panels work, selecting the right components, and optimizing installation for maximum efficiency, you can harness the power of the sun to achieve energy independence. Remember, maintenance and regular monitoring are key to keeping your system running smoothly for years.

As you continue building your off-grid lifestyle, integrating solar power with other renewable energy sources can further enhance your self-sufficiency and resilience. In the next chapter, we'll explore wind power systems in depth, examining how they can complement solar setups and provide additional energy stability.

Chapter 4: Wind Power for Homesteads

Wind power is an excellent option for homesteads, particularly those located in areas with consistent wind patterns. It offers a reliable and renewable energy source that can complement solar systems, ensuring that your off-grid setup continues to generate electricity even when sunlight is unavailable. Understanding the basics of wind energy, how wind turbines work, and how to choose and install the right system for your property are key steps in making the most of wind power.

Basics of Wind Energy

Wind energy harnesses the natural movement of air and converts it into mechanical and then electrical energy. Wind turbines are the devices used to capture and convert this energy. Here's how the process works:

How Wind Turbines Generate Power:

A wind turbine consists of blades, a rotor, a nacelle (which houses the gearbox and generator), and a tower. As wind blows, it causes the turbine blades to spin. The rotor, connected to these blades, spins as well.

The spinning rotor turns a shaft inside the nacelle, which is connected to a generator. This generator then converts the mechanical energy from the rotor into electrical energy.

Wind turbines generate Alternating Current (AC) electricity, which is suitable for most household appliances. If you are using an off-grid setup with batteries (which store Direct Current (DC)), an inverter is needed to convert the AC into DC for storage, and then back into AC when the power is used.

Turbine Types:

Horizontal Axis Wind Turbines (HAWT): These are the most common type, characterized by their horizontal rotating axis. They are generally more efficient and are suitable for larger-scale installations where space and strong wind are available.

Vertical Axis Wind Turbines (VAWT): These have a vertical rotating axis and are typically smaller. They work well in urban or small-space environments and perform better in turbulent wind conditions, though they are usually less efficient overall.

Key Wind Energy Terminology:

Cut-In Speed: The minimum wind speed required for a turbine to start generating power (usually around 6-9 mph).

Rated Wind Speed: The speed at which the turbine generates its maximum power output.

Cut-Out Speed: The speed beyond which the turbine shuts down to prevent damage, often at around 55 mph.

Choosing the Right Wind Turbine for Your Property

Selecting the appropriate wind turbine for your homestead involves understanding your location's wind patterns, evaluating your power needs, and choosing a system that matches those requirements. Here are the critical steps for making the right choice:

Evaluating Your Wind Resource:

The first step is to determine if your property has enough consistent wind to make a turbine effective. Ideally, wind speeds should average 9-12 mph (15-19 km/h) or higher. You can measure wind speed using an anemometer, a device that records wind speed and direction over time.

It's important to collect data over a period of several months to get an accurate picture of the wind conditions throughout different seasons. If you find that wind speeds are below the minimum required, it may not be cost-effective to invest in wind power alone.

Sizing the Wind Turbine:

Wind turbines come in various sizes, typically ranging from small-scale systems (400W to 1kW) suitable for charging batteries and small appliances, to medium-scale turbines (1kW to 10kW) that can power entire homes or multiple buildings.

The size you choose should depend on your average wind speeds and your energy needs. A homestead with moderate power requirements (e.g., 3-5 kWh per day) might require a turbine rated between 2kW to 5kW, assuming consistent wind speeds.

For homesteads combining solar and wind, smaller turbines (1kW-2kW) can work effectively to supplement power during low-sunlight periods, particularly at night when winds tend to be stronger.

Understanding Tower Height and Location:

The height of your wind turbine is crucial, as wind speeds increase with height. A standard recommendation is to place the turbine tower at least 30 feet above any obstacles (e.g., trees, buildings) within a 300-foot radius. Taller towers can capture stronger and more consistent winds, leading to higher energy output.

When selecting the installation site, prioritize open areas like hilltops, fields, or clearings where the wind is least obstructed. Ensure the tower is anchored securely, as higher towers need to withstand more force from the wind.

Installation and Setup of Wind Power Systems

Installing a wind turbine system on your homestead involves several stages, from site preparation to erecting the tower and configuring the system for energy storage and use. Here's a detailed guide on how to install your wind power system:

Preparing the Site:

Clear the area of any obstacles, and choose a location that provides ample space for the tower base and guy wires (if needed). Wind turbines often come with specific guidelines for setback distances, which dictate how far the tower should be from structures and property boundaries to prevent damage in case of collapse.

Ensure that the ground is stable enough to support the turbine's weight and withstand wind forces. Depending on the soil type, you may need to pour a concrete foundation for the tower.

Erecting the Tower:

There are two main types of towers: guyed towers, which are supported by cables anchored to the ground, and self-supporting towers, which are more rigid and stand on their own. Guyed towers are typically more economical but require more space for the guy wires.

Assemble the tower according to the manufacturer's instructions, ensuring all connections are secure. For larger systems, you may need professional assistance or machinery to lift the tower into place safely.

Wiring the System:

Connect the wind turbine to a charge controller, which regulates the electricity flow to the battery bank. This device ensures that the batteries are not overcharged and maintains an optimal charging rate.

From the charge controller, wire the system to your battery bank for energy storage. Make sure to use weather-resistant cables and protect connections to prevent wear from exposure to wind and rain.

Finally, connect the battery bank to an inverter that converts DC into AC power, making it usable for household appliances. It's critical to size your inverter based on the maximum output of the turbine and your peak energy demands.

Safety Precautions:

Ensure the tower is grounded properly to protect against lightning strikes, which can cause significant damage to wind turbines. Install lightning arresters and use proper grounding rods to direct the electricity safely into the ground.

Equip the turbine with a manual brake or shutoff switch, allowing you to stop the turbine during extreme weather conditions or maintenance periods. This is essential for preventing damage from high winds that exceed the turbine's rated cut-out speed.

Maximizing Efficiency: Tips for Optimal Performance

To get the most out of your wind power system, it's important to understand how to maximize efficiency through proper placement, maintenance, and system adjustments.

Monitoring Wind Performance:

Installing a wind monitoring system can help you track wind speeds and turbine performance over time. Data from these systems allows you to adjust the turbine's angle or height to capture optimal wind flow.

Use a data logger to record wind patterns, including peak and low speeds, and compare these with energy output to identify any discrepancies or opportunities for improvement.

Routine Maintenance:

Regular inspections of the turbine's blades, tower, and wiring are essential to keep the system operating efficiently. Blades can accumulate dirt, ice, or debris, which affects their aerodynamics and efficiency. Clean them periodically and check for any cracks or signs of wear.

Lubricate moving parts like the rotor and bearings to minimize friction and ensure smooth operation. Review manufacturer guidelines for recommended maintenance schedules and tasks specific to your turbine model.

Adjusting for Seasonal Changes:

Wind conditions can vary significantly between seasons, so adjusting your turbine for optimal capture during these changes is important. For example, in areas with higher winter wind speeds, you may want to adjust the turbine's angle to better capture lower-angle winds.

For homesteads that experience frequent storms or high winds, ensure the turbine's shutoff mechanism is functioning properly to protect the system during extreme weather.

Troubleshooting Common Wind Power Issues

Even with proper setup and maintenance, wind power systems can encounter issues that affect their performance. Here are some common problems and troubleshooting tips:

Low Energy Output:

If your turbine is producing less energy than expected, check for obstructions like trees or buildings that may be blocking the wind. Over time, vegetation can grow and impact wind flow, so regular site assessments are necessary.

Another common cause of low output is a misaligned turbine. Use a wind vane or monitoring device to ensure the turbine is positioned to capture the prevailing wind direction accurately. Adjust the yaw mechanism (which orients the turbine) as needed.

Turbine Noise and Vibration:

Excessive noise or vibration is usually a sign of a mechanical issue, such as loose bolts, worn bearings, or blade imbalance. Inspect all moving parts and tighten or replace components as needed.

Vibration can also indicate that the tower is not properly anchored. Check the foundation and guy wires to ensure stability, especially after high-wind events.

Battery and Charge Controller Issues:

If your batteries are not holding charge, it may be due to improper connections or an underperforming charge controller. Inspect the wiring between the turbine, charge controller, and batteries for damage or corrosion. Clean terminals and connections to ensure proper energy flow.

Test the charge controller to confirm it is regulating the voltage correctly. If the controller is malfunctioning, it may need to be replaced to prevent overcharging or undercharging the batteries.

Hybrid Wind-Solar Systems: Integrating Wind with Solar Power

For many off-grid homesteaders, combining wind and solar power creates a more balanced and reliable energy system. Hybrid systems can capitalize on the strengths of both energy sources, ensuring that power is available regardless of weather conditions.

Benefits of Hybrid Systems:

Solar panels generate energy during daylight hours, while wind turbines can produce power at night when winds are often stronger. By combining these two sources, you can achieve more consistent energy production and reduce reliance on battery storage.

Hybrid setups also improve resilience, as they reduce the risk of complete power loss if one source becomes temporarily unavailable (e.g., during prolonged cloudy weather for solar or low-wind periods for turbines).

System Integration:

To integrate wind and solar power, use a hybrid charge controller designed to manage multiple inputs. These controllers regulate both solar and wind energy, directing power to the battery bank efficiently.

Ensure your inverter is compatible with hybrid systems, as some inverters are specifically designed to handle combined energy sources and can manage fluctuating inputs more effectively.

Optimizing Load Management:

With a hybrid system, load management becomes more flexible. For example, energy-intensive tasks (e.g., running washing machines or powering electric tools) can be scheduled during peak solar hours or when wind speeds are high, minimizing battery drain and maximizing system efficiency.

Monitoring energy inputs from both sources allows you to optimize usage patterns, ensuring that your homestead has a continuous supply of energy.

Regulatory and Environmental Considerations

Permitting and Zoning Requirements:

Before installing a wind turbine, it's essential to check local regulations. Zoning laws may dictate the maximum height of towers or require specific setback distances from neighboring properties. Some regions also require environmental impact assessments before installation, particularly if the turbine may affect local wildlife (e.g., bird migration paths).

Applying for the necessary permits and consulting with local authorities can help you avoid legal complications later on. It's also beneficial to engage with neighbors and the community to ensure there are no objections to your installation.

Minimizing Environmental Impact:

Wind turbines can impact wildlife, particularly birds and bats. To minimize these risks, avoid installing turbines near known habitats or migration routes. Selecting a turbine model with slower blade rotation can also reduce the likelihood of harm.

In sensitive environments, using vertical axis turbines (VAWTs) may be more appropriate as they tend to be less intrusive to wildlife. VAWTs operate closer to the ground and generally rotate at lower speeds, making them a safer option for areas with high bird activity.

Future-Proofing Your Wind Power System

Upgrading Components:

As technology advances, newer turbine models and control systems become available. Keeping your system up-to-date can improve efficiency and output. For example, modern turbines with smart features can automatically adjust blade pitch to optimize performance based on real-time wind conditions.

When considering upgrades, evaluate the cost-benefit of retrofitting your existing tower and turbine versus investing in a new model. Often, incremental upgrades like advanced monitoring systems or more efficient charge controllers can enhance your system without major reinvestments.

Expanding Your System:

If your homestead's energy needs grow, scaling up your wind system is an option. This might involve installing a second turbine or increasing the height of your existing tower to capture higher wind speeds. Ensure that any expansion plans are compatible with your current setup, including battery capacity and charge controller capabilities.

For hybrid systems, adding additional solar panels or incorporating other energy sources like micro-hydro can create a more robust and adaptable power system.

Conclusion: Building a Resilient Wind Power System for Your Homestead

Wind power offers off-grid homesteaders a versatile and sustainable energy option, particularly when paired with other renewable sources like solar. By understanding how wind turbines work, selecting the right system for your property, and properly installing and maintaining the equipment, you can harness the power of the wind to achieve energy independence.

Whether you choose wind power as a standalone system or as part of a hybrid setup, thoughtful planning and consistent maintenance will ensure a reliable source of energy that supports your off-grid lifestyle for years to come. In the next chapter, we will explore hydro power systems, diving into the specifics of designing and installing micro-hydro setups that use water flow as a continuous and efficient energy source.

Chapter 5: Setting Up a Hydro Power System

Hydropower is one of the most reliable and efficient forms of renewable energy, particularly for off-grid homesteads located near flowing water sources like rivers, streams, or creeks. By harnessing the natural movement of water, a micro-hydro system can generate consistent electricity, often with less maintenance than solar or wind systems. This chapter will guide you through the basics of hydroelectric power, how to evaluate your site for viability, and the steps to build and maintain a micro-hydro system for your small-scale energy needs.

Hydroelectric Basics: How Hydro Power Works

Hydroelectric power relies on the flow and pressure of water to turn a turbine, which converts the kinetic energy of the moving water into mechanical energy. This mechanical energy is then transformed into electrical energy using a generator. The basic components of a micro-hydro system include:

Intake and Penstock:

The intake is the point where water is diverted from the stream or river into the system. This intake should be positioned where water flow is steady and continuous throughout the year.

The penstock is a pipe that directs water from the intake down to the turbine. The pressure of water flowing through the penstock is what drives the turbine blades. The length, diameter, and angle of the penstock are all crucial for maximizing energy output.

Turbine:

The turbine is the component that converts water flow into rotational energy. There are several types of turbines, including Pelton wheels (ideal for high-head, low-flow sites) and Kaplan turbines (suitable for low-head, high-flow sites). Choosing the right turbine depends on your specific water source and terrain.

Generator and Control System:

The turbine is connected to a generator that converts mechanical energy into electricity. In a micro-hydro setup, this is typically a small AC or DC generator designed to handle variable water flows.

A control system regulates the electricity output, directing power to your battery bank or grid and managing fluctuations in water flow to prevent damage to the turbine and generator.

Battery Bank and Inverter:

In off-grid systems, a battery bank stores the electricity generated by the turbine, ensuring power is available even when water flow decreases or when demand is higher than supply. An inverter converts the DC power stored in the batteries into AC power for household use.

Site Assessment for Hydro Power: Evaluating Water Flow and Terrain

Setting up a micro-hydro system requires a thorough site assessment to determine if your location can support a viable and efficient system. Two key factors in this evaluation are water flow and head:

Measuring Water Flow:

Water flow, measured in cubic feet per second (CFS) or liters per second (LPS), is the volume of water passing a given point over time. To measure flow, you can use a simple method called the cross-sectional area method:

Measure the width of the stream at its narrowest point and the average depth at multiple points.

Multiply the width by the average depth to get the cross-sectional area.

Using a floating object, measure how long it takes to travel a set distance downstream. Multiply the speed (distance/time) by the cross-sectional area to estimate flow.

Accurate flow measurement is essential for determining how much power the system can generate. It's important to collect data across different seasons, as flow can vary significantly between wet and dry periods.

Calculating Head:

The head is the vertical drop of water from the intake to the turbine. It directly impacts the pressure and energy potential of the system; the greater the head, the more energy can be generated. You can measure head using simple surveying equipment like a level and ruler or more advanced tools like a transit level.

Divide the total height drop into smaller sections if the terrain is uneven, measuring each section and summing the values for an accurate total head. Low-head systems typically require a high flow rate to be effective, while high-head systems can generate more power with less water flow.

Assessing Site Terrain:

Terrain plays a significant role in hydro system design. Steep slopes with consistent water flow are ideal, as they provide the necessary head and minimize the length of the penstock. Flat or gently sloping terrain can also be used, but these setups often require larger pipes and more construction work to maintain water pressure.

Consider the accessibility of the site, as you will need to transport equipment like turbines, piping, and generators. Additionally, plan for potential challenges such as soil erosion or landslides, which could damage the system over time.

Legal and Environmental Considerations

Before installing a micro-hydro system, it's essential to review local regulations and environmental impacts:

Permitting Requirements:

In many regions, diverting water for hydroelectric use requires a permit. Authorities may have regulations to protect fish habitats, water quality, and downstream water rights. Failing to comply can result in fines or forced removal of your system.

Consulting with local water authorities or environmental agencies is advisable before beginning construction. Some areas also require an Environmental Impact Assessment (EIA) to ensure your system doesn't negatively impact the ecosystem.

Minimizing Environmental Impact:

It's important to design your intake to minimize disruption to aquatic life. Installing a screen or filter at the intake point can prevent fish and debris from entering the system. Consider using a bypass flow that allows water to continue flowing naturally in parts of the stream to support local wildlife.

Additionally, ensure that the outflow of your system returns water to the stream in a manner that prevents erosion and doesn't disturb the natural watercourse.

Building a Micro-Hydro System for Small-Scale Power Needs

If your site assessment confirms sufficient flow and head, you can begin designing and building your micro-hydro system. The following steps outline the process:

Choosing the Right Turbine:

Select a turbine based on the characteristics of your site:

Pelton Wheel Turbines are effective for high-head, low-flow sites. They operate by directing water jets onto cups (buckets) mounted on a wheel, converting the pressure of the falling water into rotational energy.

Crossflow Turbines work well for medium-head, medium-flow sites and are robust, making them suitable for homesteads where maintenance access may be limited.

Kaplan and Propeller Turbines are ideal for low-head, high-flow sites. These turbines are submerged in water and use propeller-like blades to generate power from fast-moving water.

Constructing the Intake and Penstock:

The intake should be placed at a point where the water flow is strong and consistent. Install a debris screen at the intake to prevent blockages in the penstock and damage to the turbine.

The penstock needs to be built with durable, weather-resistant materials, such as PVC or metal pipes. Ensure the pipe diameter is sufficient to maintain flow pressure; undersized penstocks can restrict water flow, reducing efficiency.

Secure the penstock along the terrain, using brackets or concrete footings to prevent movement and leaks. For steeper slopes, additional anchoring may be necessary.

Installing the Turbine and Generator:

Position the turbine at the bottom of the penstock where the water's velocity and pressure are highest. Ensure the turbine's location is secure and protected from debris or flooding.

Connect the turbine to the generator using a coupling or drive shaft. Depending on your setup, the generator can be mounted directly on the turbine or placed separately. Test the alignment to ensure that the rotation is smooth and efficient.

Once the turbine is operational, connect the generator output to the charge controller and battery bank. The charge controller regulates the voltage and prevents overcharging, ensuring stable energy storage.

Setting Up the Electrical System:

Similar to solar and wind systems, the energy produced by a hydro system is typically stored in batteries for later use. Connect the generator output to the battery bank using the charge controller to manage energy flow.

Install an inverter to convert DC electricity from the batteries into AC power. Size the inverter based on your anticipated energy consumption, ensuring it can handle peak loads. In hydro systems, the inverter should also have surge protection to handle fluctuations caused by variations in water flow.

Maintaining a Micro-Hydro System

A well-maintained micro-hydro system can provide reliable energy for decades. Here are the key maintenance tasks and strategies:

Regular Inspection of the Intake and Penstock:

The intake and penstock are vulnerable to blockages from debris, leaves, or sediment buildup. Inspect these components regularly, especially after heavy rains or seasonal changes that may cause flooding. Clean out debris screens to ensure a continuous flow of water to the turbine.

Check the penstock for leaks, as even small leaks can significantly reduce the efficiency of the system. Reinforce or replace damaged sections as needed to maintain optimal pressure.

Turbine Maintenance:

Periodically inspect the turbine for signs of wear or damage. Clean the turbine's blades to remove any algae or sediment that may accumulate over time. If the turbine is located in a high-debris area, consider installing additional protective measures like baffles or more robust filters.

Lubricate the moving parts, such as bearings and shafts, to reduce friction and extend the lifespan of the turbine. Follow the manufacturer's recommendations for lubrication intervals and the type of lubricant to use.

Generator and Electrical System Checkups:

The generator is a crucial component that converts mechanical energy into electricity. Ensure it remains clean and dry, as exposure to moisture can cause corrosion and electrical faults. Check the wiring and connections for signs of wear and replace any damaged components promptly.

Test the charge controller periodically to verify that it is regulating voltage correctly. Battery health should also be monitored, checking for proper charge levels and inspecting for corrosion on terminals.

Troubleshooting Common Hydro Power Issues

Even with careful design and maintenance, micro-hydro systems can encounter issues. Knowing how to troubleshoot common problems ensures your system stays operational:

Reduced Power Output:

If your system is generating less power than expected, inspect the intake for blockages or debris that may be reducing water flow. Check the penstock for leaks or clogs, as these can also diminish pressure and flow.

Ensure the turbine is operating smoothly. If it appears sluggish, clean the blades and check for any signs of mechanical wear. Adjust the turbine's position if water flow has shifted due to natural changes in the stream or terrain.

Battery and Charge Controller Issues:

If batteries are not charging properly, check the connections between the generator, charge controller, and batteries. Clean terminals and check for loose connections that may be disrupting energy flow.

Test the charge controller's output to confirm it matches the voltage expected from the generator. If the controller is not functioning correctly, it may need to be recalibrated or replaced.

Penstock Damage or Leaks:

Penstocks are exposed to natural elements and can suffer from cracks or wear over time. Regularly inspect the entire length for signs of damage. Small leaks can often be patched with waterproof sealant, while larger issues may require replacing sections of the pipe.

Scaling and Upgrading Your Hydro Power System

Micro-hydro systems are inherently scalable, meaning you can increase their capacity or upgrade components as your homestead's energy needs grow.

Increasing Capacity:

If your water source supports higher flow or head than your current system utilizes, you may expand by installing additional turbines or increasing the diameter of the penstock. This can boost power output without significant redesign.

Adding multiple turbines in parallel or series allows you to generate more electricity, though this setup requires additional control mechanisms to balance the load between generators and battery storage.

Integrating with Other Renewable Systems:

Hydro systems often pair well with solar or wind setups. A hybrid system allows for more consistent energy production, as solar panels or wind turbines can supplement power during periods of low water flow (e.g., dry seasons).

Using a hybrid charge controller helps manage inputs from multiple sources, ensuring the energy is efficiently stored and distributed throughout your system.

Adopting New Technologies:

Advances in micro-hydro technology, such as improved turbine designs or smart control systems, offer opportunities to enhance the efficiency of your setup. Consider upgrading to a smart inverter or a variable flow controller that automatically adjusts turbine speed and output based on water conditions.

Conclusion: Harnessing Hydro Power for Off-Grid Living

Micro-hydro power offers a reliable and efficient solution for homesteaders with access to flowing water. By understanding the basics of hydroelectric systems, properly assessing your site, and building a robust setup, you can create a continuous energy source that supports your off-grid lifestyle year-round.

With proper maintenance and occasional upgrades, a micro-hydro system can last for decades, providing a dependable foundation for energy independence. In the next chapter, we will transition into the essentials of planning your off-grid garden, including selecting crops, permaculture techniques, and ensuring a year-round harvest.

Chapter 6: Planning Your Off-Grid Garden

An off-grid garden is a vital element for achieving self-sufficiency and food security. Growing your own fruits, vegetables, and herbs not only provides fresh, nutritious produce but also reduces your reliance on grocery stores and commercial supply chains. A successful garden requires careful planning, especially when it comes to selecting crops that are compatible with your local climate and designing systems that maximize efficiency. This chapter will guide you through choosing crops for year-round growth, setting up a permaculture garden, and maintaining soil health through crop rotation and the use of natural fertilizers.

Selecting Crops for Year-Round Growth and Climate Compatibility

Choosing the right crops for your off-grid garden is critical. Your selections should be based on the local climate, soil type, and the length of the growing season in your area. The goal is to create a garden that provides a continuous supply of food throughout the year.

Understanding Your Climate Zone:

Your garden's success largely depends on how well you understand your USDA Hardiness Zone or the equivalent climate zone in your region. These zones help determine which plants will thrive based on average annual temperatures and frost dates.

Knowing your growing season length is also essential. Short-season climates might require cold-hardy and fast-maturing varieties, while regions with longer growing periods can support a wider range of crops.

Year-Round Crop Selection:

Cool-Season Crops: These are crops that grow well in cooler temperatures, such as lettuce, kale, spinach, peas, broccoli, and carrots. Plant these in early spring or fall for harvest before or after the peak summer heat.

Warm-Season Crops: Crops like tomatoes, peppers, beans, squash, and corn thrive in warmer weather. These should be planted after the last frost date in your area and can be harvested during the summer months.

Perennial Plants: Incorporating perennials such as asparagus, rhubarb, berry bushes, and fruit trees adds stability to your garden, as these crops provide food year after year without needing replanting. They are also ideal for off-grid homesteads because they establish deep root systems that improve soil health and water retention.

Extending the Growing Season:

Using structures like cold frames, hoop houses, and greenhouses can help extend your growing season, allowing you to start planting earlier in the spring and continue harvesting later into the fall. Greenhouses, in particular, can provide a controlled environment for sensitive plants that need protection from frost.

Mulching and row covers are additional techniques that insulate soil and plants, keeping them warm and protecting them from extreme weather. These methods are simple yet effective for off-grid gardeners who want to maximize their harvests without relying on external energy sources.

Designing a Permaculture Garden for Efficiency and Sustainability

Permaculture is a gardening approach that focuses on creating a self-sustaining ecosystem. By mimicking natural systems and working with the environment rather than against it, a permaculture garden can produce abundant food while conserving resources like water and soil. Here's how to design an efficient and sustainable permaculture garden for your off-grid homestead:

Zoning Your Garden:

A permaculture garden is typically divided into zones based on the frequency of human activity and the needs of the plants. These zones help you organize your garden efficiently:

Zone 1: This is the area closest to your home, where you plant high-maintenance crops that require daily attention, such as herbs, leafy greens, and vegetables harvested frequently.

Zone 2: This area is for larger crops like potatoes, carrots, and squash that need less frequent care. It may also include fruit bushes and small trees.

Zone 3: This is for perennials and larger fruit or nut trees that need minimal maintenance. It's further away from your living space but still accessible for occasional care and harvest.

Zone 4 and beyond: These areas are often used for forest gardening, livestock, or resource gathering, like firewood, and may not require daily visits.

Creating Plant Guilds:

A key concept in permaculture is the plant guild, a group of plants that benefit each other when grown together. For example, a fruit tree guild may include the tree itself, nitrogen-fixing plants (like clover) to enrich the soil, ground cover plants (like strawberries) to retain moisture, and aromatic herbs (like chives) to repel pests. These groupings work symbiotically, enhancing soil health and productivity.

Incorporating companion planting techniques can also enhance your garden's efficiency. For example, planting basil near tomatoes can repel pests and improve growth, while corn, beans, and squash (known as the Three Sisters) grow in harmony, each providing unique benefits to the others.

Water Management and Conservation:

Designing your garden with water conservation in mind is crucial, especially for off-grid homesteads. Install swales (shallow ditches) on contour lines to capture and retain rainwater, directing it slowly into the soil. This technique reduces erosion and keeps the garden hydrated naturally.

Use mulching extensively to keep soil moisture levels stable. Mulches made from straw, leaves, or grass clippings help reduce evaporation, suppress weeds, and add organic matter as they decompose. For areas with more intensive water needs, consider building a rainwater catchment system to store water for irrigation.

Maximizing Vertical Space:

Vertical gardening can maximize space and increase yield, especially for small gardens. Use trellises, arbors, and fences to grow climbing plants like beans, peas, cucumbers, and grapes. Vertical gardening also improves air circulation, reducing the risk of fungal diseases.

Incorporating structures like stacked planters or wall-mounted gardens in Zone 1 allows you to grow more herbs and smaller vegetables close to your home without taking up ground space.

Designing for Wildlife and Pollinators:

A healthy garden ecosystem relies on attracting beneficial insects, pollinators, and other wildlife. Plant a variety of flowering plants like marigolds, lavender, and echinacea to attract bees and butterflies, which are essential for pollination.

Include birdhouses or bat boxes to provide habitats for animals that control pests naturally. By creating a balanced ecosystem, you reduce the need for chemical interventions and promote biodiversity.

Soil Health, Crop Rotation, and Natural Fertilizers

The foundation of any successful garden is healthy soil. Maintaining and improving soil fertility ensures that your plants receive the necessary nutrients and that the garden remains productive for years. Here's how to build and maintain soil health through crop rotation and natural fertilizers:

Building Healthy Soil:

Start by testing your soil to understand its pH levels and nutrient composition. Most vegetables prefer slightly acidic to neutral soil (pH 6-7). Based on the test results, you can amend the soil with organic materials such as lime (to raise pH) or sulfur (to lower pH) as needed.

Composting is an essential practice for enriching soil naturally. Collect kitchen scraps, grass clippings, leaves, and manure to create a nutrient-rich compost. Compost improves soil structure, retains moisture, and provides a balanced mix of essential nutrients for plants.

Crop Rotation:

Crop rotation is the practice of alternating crops in different garden areas each season to prevent soil depletion and reduce pest buildup. For example, rotate legumes (like beans) with leafy greens (like lettuce) and root crops (like carrots). Legumes fix nitrogen in the soil, while leafy greens and root crops utilize those nutrients differently.

Use a four-year rotation plan for best results:

Year 1: Plant legumes (beans, peas) to add nitrogen to the soil.

Year 2: Follow with leafy greens (lettuce, spinach) that benefit from the enriched soil.

Year 3: Plant root crops (carrots, beets) that use different nutrients.

Year 4: Rotate in fruiting crops (tomatoes, peppers) and then start the cycle again.

Natural Fertilizers and Soil Amendments:

Fertilizing naturally is vital for off-grid homesteads to maintain soil health without relying on synthetic chemicals. Common natural fertilizers include:

Manure: Chicken, cow, or goat manure is rich in nitrogen but should be composted before use to reduce its acidity and prevent burning plants.

Bone Meal: This is a great source of phosphorus, essential for root development and flowering. It can be sprinkled directly into planting holes or incorporated into the soil.

Wood Ash: If you have a wood-burning stove, the ash can be added to the garden as a source of potassium. Use it sparingly, as it can raise soil pH if applied in excess.

Other soil amendments like worm castings (from vermicomposting) and fish emulsion provide a balanced nutrient boost and improve soil structure.

Green Manures and Cover Crops:

Planting cover crops such as clover, rye, or vetch during off-seasons can prevent soil erosion, suppress weeds, and add organic matter when tilled back into the soil. These crops also fix nitrogen, enriching the soil for the next planting season.

Incorporating green manures (crops grown specifically to be turned back into the soil) is another effective way to boost soil health. For example, planting alfalfa or buckwheat in fall and tilling it in before spring planting can significantly improve soil texture and nutrient levels.

Managing Pests and Diseases Naturally

Maintaining a healthy off-grid garden involves proactive pest and disease management. Avoiding chemical pesticides is important for sustainability and soil health. Here are some natural methods to manage garden pests:

Companion Planting for Pest Control:

Pairing certain plants together can help repel pests. For instance, planting marigolds with tomatoes deters nematodes, while basil can repel mosquitoes and flies when grown near other vegetables.

Interplant garlic and onions around susceptible crops to naturally deter pests like aphids and caterpillars. Aromatic herbs such as rosemary and thyme are also effective as deterrents.

Physical Barriers:

Use netting or floating row covers to protect vulnerable plants from insects like cabbage worms and moths. Row covers create a physical barrier that prevents pests while still allowing sunlight and rain to reach the plants.

Install fencing or build raised beds with protective screens to keep out larger animals like deer, rabbits, or rodents that may target garden produce.

Encouraging Beneficial Insects:

Not all insects are harmful. Encourage ladybugs, hoverflies, and lacewings by planting dill, fennel, and yarrow, which attract these beneficial predators. These insects help control aphids, mites, and other pests naturally.

Avoid using broad-spectrum insecticides, even organic ones, as they can kill beneficial insects along with pests, disrupting the garden's ecosystem.

Organic Pest Sprays and Treatments:

Make your own pest sprays using ingredients like neem oil, which acts as a natural insecticide against a variety of pests without harming beneficial insects. Another option is a garlic and pepper spray that deters aphids, caterpillars, and other common pests.

Soap sprays (using mild liquid soap) can help combat soft-bodied insects like aphids and spider mites. These sprays break down the pests' outer layers, killing them without harming the plants.

Maximizing Soil Health:

Maintaining soil health is an ongoing process that involves continual observation and adjustments based on your garden's needs:

Testing and Monitoring Soil Regularly:

Conduct regular soil tests to check for nutrient deficiencies or pH imbalances. These tests will guide you in adjusting soil amendments to maintain optimal growing conditions. Off-grid homesteaders can invest in affordable soil testing kits or send samples to local agricultural extension offices for detailed analysis.

Practicing No-Till Gardening:

No-till gardening involves planting crops without disturbing the soil structure. This method protects beneficial microorganisms and earthworms, which play crucial roles in breaking down organic matter and maintaining soil fertility. Mulching and using compost-rich soil layers can help maintain soil health without tilling.

Incorporating Organic Matter:

Continuously adding compost and mulch to the garden improves soil texture, water retention, and nutrient availability. Leaves, straw, and decomposed plant material can be layered to form a rich, organic foundation for future crops.

Designing a Long-Term Planting Plan

Establishing a successful off-grid garden requires a long-term perspective. Developing a crop rotation plan, managing perennials, and preparing for changing conditions all contribute to a productive and resilient garden:

Creating a Crop Rotation Schedule:

Rotate crops every season to prevent soil nutrient depletion and minimize pest and disease cycles. Keep a garden journal to track which crops were planted in each bed and note any soil amendments or treatments used. This information helps in planning future rotations and maintaining soil health.

Managing Perennial Beds:

Perennial vegetables, herbs, and fruit trees require different management strategies than annuals. Prune fruit trees annually to maintain healthy growth and maximize yield. Divide and transplant perennial herbs, such as chives and mint, every few years to promote vigor and spread.

Add organic mulch around perennials to protect roots, retain moisture, and suppress weeds. Straw, wood chips, or leaf mulch work well for this purpose, helping to build soil structure over time.

Preparing for Seasonal and Climate Changes:

A resilient garden adapts to seasonal variations and changing climate conditions. Design your garden layout to allow for seasonal crop rotation and incorporate diverse varieties that can handle unpredictable weather patterns.

Planting heat-resistant varieties in summer and frost-tolerant crops in fall ensures productivity despite temperature extremes. For areas with drought potential, include xeriscaping techniques like drip irrigation or the use of drought-resistant plants in garden borders.

Conclusion: Building a Productive Off-Grid Garden

Establishing an off-grid garden that provides year-round produce and supports your self-sufficient lifestyle is a rewarding and ongoing process. By carefully selecting climate-compatible crops, designing a permaculture system that maximizes efficiency, and maintaining soil health through natural methods, you can create a garden that thrives without the need for external inputs.

In the next chapter, we'll explore raising livestock for food and resources, covering everything from choosing the right animals to building sustainable enclosures and managing feed and breeding.

Chapter 7: Raising Livestock for Food and Resources

Raising livestock is a crucial component of an off-grid lifestyle, providing essential food products and valuable resources like eggs, milk, meat, and wool. Selecting the right animals for your homestead requires careful consideration of your needs, available space, climate, and resources. This chapter will guide you through choosing chickens, goats, and cows—three of the most versatile and productive animals for homesteaders. We'll also cover essential aspects of housing, feeding, and breeding these animals, as well as how to utilize their products sustainably.

Choosing the Right Animals for Your Homestead

The first step in setting up a livestock system is choosing animals that align with your goals and the conditions of your homestead. Chickens, goats, and cows are common choices because they are relatively easy to manage and offer multiple benefits.

Chickens: The Versatile Starter Animal

Chickens are often the first livestock choice for homesteaders due to their small space requirements, low maintenance, and ability to provide both eggs and meat. They are adaptable to a variety of climates and can be integrated into garden systems to control pests and fertilize soil.

Egg Layers vs. Meat Birds: When choosing chickens, decide whether you want them primarily for egg production or meat. Layers such as Leghorns and Rhode Island Reds are prolific egg producers, while broiler breeds like Cornish Cross are raised for meat. Dual-purpose breeds, such as Plymouth Rocks or Orpingtons, offer both eggs and meat, making them versatile options for small homesteads.

Goats: Milk and More

Goats are ideal for homesteads with limited space or rough terrain, as they are hardy and adaptable animals that can thrive in conditions where cows may not. They are excellent sources of milk and can also be raised for meat and fiber (in the case of breeds like Angora).

Dairy Breeds: Breeds like Nubian and Alpine goats are known for their milk production. Goat milk is a valuable resource for making cheese, yogurt, and other dairy products.

Meat Breeds: Boer and Kiko goats are commonly raised for meat. They grow quickly and have good feed conversion rates, making them efficient livestock for small-scale meat production.

Cows: The Traditional Homestead Animal

Cows are larger animals that require more space and resources, but they are incredibly productive. Dairy cows can provide large quantities of milk daily, which can be processed into butter, cheese, and other dairy products. Beef cattle, on the other hand, are raised for meat and can supply a homestead with a significant protein source.

Dairy Breeds: Popular dairy breeds include Jersey and Holstein, known for their high milk yield and manageable temperaments. Jerseys, in particular, are preferred for their high butterfat content, which is ideal for making butter and cream-based products.

Beef Breeds: Angus and Hereford cattle are common beef breeds that are relatively hardy and efficient in converting pasture into high-quality meat.

Housing, Feeding, and Breeding Livestock

To raise healthy and productive animals, proper housing, nutrition, and breeding management are essential. Each type of livestock has specific requirements to thrive, and creating appropriate facilities and routines ensures their well-being and productivity.

Housing for Chickens, Goats, and Cows

Chickens: Chickens require a secure coop to protect them from predators and provide shelter from the elements. The coop should be well-ventilated, with nesting boxes for egg laying and perches for roosting at night. Access to an outdoor run or pasture allows chickens to forage, which contributes to their diet and overall health. A ratio of 4 square feet per chicken inside the coop and 10 square feet per bird in the run is a good guideline.

Goats: Goats need shelter that protects them from rain, wind, and cold temperatures. A small barn or shed with a fenced outdoor area for grazing is ideal. Ensure that fencing is secure and tall enough (at least 4 feet) to prevent escapes, as goats are skilled climbers. Inside the shelter, provide bedding like straw or hay and keep the space clean to reduce the risk of disease.

Cows: Cows require larger barns or shelters, particularly for dairy breeds that need protection during milking. A clean, dry space with sufficient ventilation is crucial. Outdoor pasture space is essential for grazing, as cows need to move and forage naturally. The amount of land needed varies, but typically 1-2 acres per cow is recommended for rotational grazing.

Feeding Requirements and Foraging

Chickens: Chickens thrive on a mix of commercial feed, kitchen scraps, and foraged insects or greens. A balanced diet includes grains, protein sources (like insects or worms), and calcium (through oyster shells or crushed eggshells) for strong eggshell production. Supplement their diet with fresh greens, such as clover or spinach, and allow them to free-range when possible for additional nutrients.

Goats: Goats are browsers rather than grazers, preferring to eat shrubs, leaves, and small trees. They require a balanced diet of forage supplemented with hay, minerals, and grain (for pregnant or lactating does). Providing a mineral block ensures they receive essential nutrients like calcium and phosphorus, important for bone health and milk production.

Cows: Cows require substantial amounts of forage, typically in the form of pasture grass or hay. For dairy cows, additional grain may be needed to support milk production. Ensure cows have access to clean water at all times, as dehydration can significantly affect both growth and milk yield. Rotational grazing practices allow pastures to recover and prevent overgrazing.

Breeding and Reproduction

Chickens: For egg production, hens do not need a rooster; however, if you plan to hatch chicks, a rooster is essential. Roosters also provide protection for free-ranging flocks. Hens typically start laying eggs at around 5-6 months of age, and their productivity peaks for the first two years. For breeding, ensure that the ratio of roosters to hens is balanced (typically one rooster for every 8-10 hens) to prevent stress and injury.

Goats: Goats typically breed once a year, with a gestation period of about 150 days. Does (female goats) are usually bred in the fall for spring births. Keeping a buck (male goat) on-site makes breeding more convenient, but they require separate housing to avoid aggressive behavior and odor issues. If you choose to borrow or rent a buck for breeding, ensure it is healthy and disease-free.

Cows: Cows are generally bred annually, with a gestation period of approximately 283 days. Artificial insemination (AI) is a common practice for dairy cows, allowing for controlled breeding and genetic improvement without the need for a bull. However, keeping a bull on-site can be beneficial for smaller herds, provided there are secure facilities to manage the bull safely. For beef cattle, natural breeding is often used, and bulls are integrated into herds during breeding seasons.

Utilizing Animal Products: Eggs, Milk, Meat, and Wool

Maximizing the resources your livestock provide is key to off-grid self-sufficiency. Proper management allows you to sustainably harvest eggs, milk, meat, and other products without depleting resources.

Egg Production and Care

Chickens can lay eggs almost daily, depending on the breed and conditions. Collect eggs daily to maintain cleanliness and prevent hens from developing brooding behavior, which can reduce laying productivity.

To extend the egg-laying season during winter months when daylight is limited, provide supplemental lighting in the coop. A low-wattage bulb set on a timer to provide 14 hours of light per day can stimulate laying. Ensure the coop remains warm, as extreme cold can reduce egg production.

Surplus eggs can be preserved through techniques like pickling, water glassing (an old method using sodium silicate), or by freezing eggs for long-term storage.

Milk Production and Processing

Goats and cows can be milked daily, with dairy goats typically yielding 1-2 gallons of milk per day and cows producing much more—between 3 and 6 gallons depending on the breed and feeding regimen. Regular milking is essential to maintain lactation, so establish a routine.

Fresh milk can be consumed directly, but many homesteaders choose to process it into products like cheese, butter, and yogurt. For cheese, goats' milk is particularly well-suited, with soft cheeses like chèvre being simple to make at home. Milk processing requires basic equipment, such as a churn for butter or molds for cheese.

Pasteurization, while not required, is recommended for safety, especially if the milk is shared or sold. Heat the milk to 161°F (72°C) for 15 seconds, then cool it quickly to preserve freshness.

Meat Production and Processing

Raising chickens for meat involves selecting fast-growing breeds like Cornish Cross. Meat birds are usually ready for processing at 6-8 weeks of age. Ensure humane processing methods and set up a designated area for butchering, plucking, and dressing the birds.

Goat meat, known as chevon or cabrito (young goat), is a valuable protein source that's lean and flavorful. Goats are typically butchered at 6-12 months, depending on the breed and purpose (e.g., young tender meat vs. mature, larger cuts). Processing goats requires facilities for humane slaughter, skinning, and meat preparation.

For beef production, cows are generally raised to 1.5-2 years before processing. Rotational grazing ensures they maintain a healthy weight gain. Building a relationship with a local butcher or learning the skills of butchery can provide significant savings and ensure that every part of the animal is utilized efficiently.

Using Wool and Other Animal Byproducts

If you raise fiber goats (like Angoras) or sheep, wool production can be an additional resource. Wool is sheared once or twice a year and can be spun into yarn or felted for crafts. Processing wool involves washing, carding (combing fibers), and spinning, which can be done by hand or with simple machines like a drop spindle.

Cowhides and goat skins can be tanned to create leather for clothing, tools, or trade. Tanning requires space and time but is a valuable skill for making durable off-grid resources.

Value-Added Products and Sustainability

Homesteaders can increase self-sufficiency and generate income by creating value-added products from livestock:

Preserved Meats and Dairy:

Smoking and curing meats are traditional ways to extend shelf life and add flavor. Goats and cattle provide ample opportunities for creating jerky, smoked cuts, and sausages. Smoking can be done using a simple smokehouse made from local materials or an existing structure.

Dairy products like hard cheeses and fermented milk (such as kefir) can be stored long-term, providing nutrition when fresh milk is less available. Curing and aging cheeses in a cool, stable environment (e.g., a root cellar) adds longevity and flavor.

Manure Management and Composting:

Livestock produce a significant amount of manure, which is an excellent natural fertilizer. Chickens, goats, and cows each provide different manure types that can be composted and used to enrich garden soil.

Chicken manure is high in nitrogen but needs to be composted for 6-12 months before use to prevent burning plants. Goat and cow manure are milder and can be added directly to compost piles. A three-bin composting system allows you to manage manure and kitchen waste efficiently, providing a continuous supply of organic matter for the garden.

Feather, Bone, and Horn Utilization:

Chickens produce feathers that can be composted, used for crafts, or incorporated into pillows and other items. Cows and goats provide bones that can be boiled down to make bone broth, which is rich in nutrients, or processed into bone meal for garden fertilizer.

Horns and hooves can be crafted into tools, buttons, or decorations, adding value and ensuring that nothing goes to waste. Learning these traditional skills enhances self-sufficiency and reduces the need for external resources.

Integrating Livestock with Garden Systems:

One of the most effective ways to maximize the productivity of your homestead is by integrating livestock with your garden and land management practices:

Rotational Grazing and Land Health:

Rotational grazing involves moving livestock between pasture areas to allow forage regrowth and prevent overgrazing. This practice improves soil health, increases pasture productivity, and reduces the need for supplemental feed.

Incorporating cover crops in rotation can further enrich the soil and provide feed. Chickens can be rotated through garden beds after harvest to eat pests and turn the soil while fertilizing it with manure.

Chickens as Pest Control:

Chickens are natural pest controllers and can be deployed in gardens or orchards to manage insect populations. Allow them to roam areas after the growing season to consume pests and fertilize the soil.

Construct mobile chicken coops (often called chicken tractors) that can be moved across garden plots, allowing birds to fertilize and till without damaging crops.

Livestock and Waste Management:

Goats and cows can be used to manage overgrown areas or clear invasive plant species. Goats, in particular, are effective at clearing brush, making them valuable for maintaining property boundaries and reducing fire hazards.

Animal bedding (straw or hay mixed with manure) can be composted to create nutrient-rich material for gardening. Using livestock waste effectively contributes to a closed-loop system where resources are continuously recycled on the homestead.

Conclusion: Raising Livestock for a Sustainable Homestead

Raising livestock provides a wide range of resources that contribute to a self-sufficient lifestyle, from eggs, milk, and meat to manure and fiber. By choosing the right animals for your needs, providing proper housing and care, and learning how to utilize and manage livestock products sustainably, you can build a resilient and productive off-grid homestead.

In the next chapter, we'll move on to orchards and perennials, discussing how to establish long-term food solutions through fruit trees, berry bushes, and perennial vegetables that require minimal maintenance and provide lasting yields.

Chapter 8: Orchards and Perennials: Long-Term Food Solutions

Establishing an orchard and planting perennial crops like berry bushes and vegetables are crucial steps toward achieving long-term food security and sustainability on an off-grid homestead. Unlike annual crops, which require replanting each year, perennials provide reliable harvests over many years with minimal maintenance once they are established. This chapter covers how to plan and plant fruit trees, berry bushes, and other perennial crops for sustainable harvests, as well as strategies for maintenance, pest control, and creating a resilient and diverse orchard that supports your self-sufficiency goals.

Planting Fruit Trees and Berry Bushes for Sustainable Harvests

The first step in establishing a productive orchard is choosing the right fruit trees and berry bushes based on your climate, soil conditions, and available space. Perennials take time to establish, but once they mature, they provide reliable harvests and require far less attention than annual crops.

Choosing the Right Fruit Trees:

Climate Compatibility: Understanding your USDA Hardiness Zone (or equivalent regional classification) is critical when selecting fruit trees. For example, apples, pears, and plums are hardy choices suitable for colder regions, while citrus, figs, and pomegranates thrive in warmer climates. Choose varieties that are compatible with your specific weather patterns, including frost risk and heat tolerance.

Pollination Requirements: Many fruit trees require cross-pollination to produce fruit, meaning you may need to plant two or more compatible varieties to ensure a good yield. For example, most apple trees are not self-pollinating and require a second tree of a different variety. On the other hand, trees like peaches and citrus are typically self-pollinating and can be planted alone.

Dwarf vs. Standard Trees: Dwarf and semi-dwarf varieties are ideal for homesteads with limited space, as they grow smaller and can be pruned easily. These trees begin bearing fruit sooner than their standard counterparts, which can take several years to mature but produce more substantial yields in the long term.

Establishing Berry Bushes:

Berry bushes like blueberries, raspberries, blackberries, and currants are perfect for off-grid homesteads, as they provide abundant harvests in a relatively small space. When selecting varieties, consider factors such as soil pH requirements (e.g., blueberries prefer acidic soil) and sunlight needs.

Strawberries are another versatile perennial that can be planted as ground cover in garden beds, raised planters, or even vertical systems for maximum yield in small areas.

Planting and Spacing Guidelines:

When planting fruit trees, spacing is crucial for ensuring that each tree has enough sunlight and room to grow. As a general guideline, dwarf trees should be planted 8-10 feet apart, while standard varieties require 15-20 feet. Berry bushes typically need 3-4 feet between plants, with rows spaced 6-8 feet apart.

Dig planting holes wide enough to accommodate the tree or bush's root system without bending or crowding roots. Incorporate compost or aged manure into the soil to provide nutrients, and mulch around the base of each tree or bush to retain moisture and suppress weeds.

Creating a Multi-Layered Orchard:

To maximize space and diversity, implement a multi-layered approach in your orchard design, similar to a food forest. Incorporate different layers, such as:

Canopy Layer: Tall fruit trees like apples, pears, or chestnuts.

Understory Layer: Smaller trees and shrubs, such as plums, figs, or hazelnuts.

Ground Cover Layer: Low-growing berry bushes like strawberries or creeping herbs such as oregano and thyme.

Vine Layer: Climbing plants like grapes or kiwi vines that can grow up trellises or tree trunks.

This approach creates a more diverse and resilient system where each layer supports the others, enhancing overall productivity.

Maintenance and Pest Control for Perennial Plants

Once your orchard and perennial beds are established, regular maintenance is essential to keep the plants healthy and productive. Proper care involves pruning, soil management, and organic pest control measures.

Pruning Fruit Trees:

Pruning is critical for maintaining the health and productivity of fruit trees. It helps manage tree size, improves air circulation, and ensures sunlight reaches all parts of the tree, which is necessary for fruit production. The best time for pruning is during the dormant season (late winter to early spring) before new growth begins.

Remove any dead, damaged, or diseased branches first. Then, focus on thinning out branches that cross or grow inward, as they can hinder airflow and light penetration. Shape the tree to have a balanced structure, with a central leader (main trunk) and well-spaced scaffold branches.

Berry bushes also benefit from pruning. Raspberries and blackberries, for instance, should have old canes cut back after fruiting, leaving space for new growth. Blueberries should be pruned to remove any deadwood and to encourage healthy fruiting branches.

Managing Soil Fertility:

Maintaining soil fertility is key to ensuring long-term productivity in your orchard. Fruit trees and berry bushes benefit from an annual application of compost or aged manure in the spring to replenish nutrients. Mulching with organic material such as wood chips, straw, or leaves conserves soil moisture, suppresses weeds, and gradually adds organic matter as it decomposes.

Soil tests should be conducted every 2-3 years to monitor pH and nutrient levels. Adjust soil amendments based on test results to maintain the right balance. For example, applying sulfur can lower soil pH for blueberries, while adding lime raises pH for crops that prefer more alkaline soil.

Organic Pest Control Techniques:

Keeping pests under control in an orchard requires an integrated approach. Beneficial insects like ladybugs, lacewings, and hoverflies naturally prey on aphids, mites, and other common pests. Attract these insects by planting dill, fennel, and other flowering herbs that provide habitat and food sources.

Use physical barriers such as netting or row covers to protect berry bushes from birds or insects. For larger trees, applying sticky bands around the trunks can prevent crawling pests, like caterpillars and ants, from climbing up and infesting the canopy.

Companion planting can also help deter pests. For example, planting marigolds or nasturtiums around fruit trees repels nematodes and aphids, while garlic and chives act as natural deterrents for other insects.

Disease Management and Prevention:

Fungal diseases such as powdery mildew and apple scab can affect fruit trees and berries. Ensure proper air circulation by pruning and avoid overhead watering, which creates conditions favorable to fungi. Copper sprays or neem oil are effective organic treatments for controlling fungal infections.

Rotating mulches and keeping the base of trees and bushes clear of fallen fruit and leaves can also prevent disease buildup. Regularly inspect your orchard for signs of disease, and remove any infected plant material to stop the spread.

Planning and Implementing Crop Diversity for Resilience

A diverse orchard and perennial system is more resilient to pests, diseases, and changing climate conditions. By planning for diversity, you increase the variety of food your homestead produces and create a more stable ecosystem that supports long-term productivity.

Incorporating Diverse Varieties:

Planting multiple varieties of the same fruit, such as several types of apples or plums, ensures cross-pollination and increases resilience. Different varieties often have varying levels of disease resistance, ripening times, and tolerance to environmental stresses. This diversity helps ensure that even if one variety is affected by pests or weather, others may still thrive.

Consider adding nut trees like hazelnuts, walnuts, or pecans to further diversify your orchard. Nut trees provide valuable protein and fat sources and often require less intensive management once established.

Integrating Herbs and Medicinal Plants:

Growing herbs such as lavender, sage, and mint in your orchard creates additional layers of productivity. These herbs attract beneficial insects, deter pests, and can be harvested for culinary or medicinal uses. Comfrey is another excellent perennial that can be used as a natural mulch, fodder for livestock, or compost tea for fertilizing other plants.

Medicinal plants like echinacea, elderberry, and yarrow serve multiple functions, providing natural remedies for homestead use while supporting pollinator populations.

Forest Gardening Techniques:

Designing your orchard with forest gardening principles allows you to mimic natural ecosystems, creating a diverse and self-sustaining environment. This approach focuses on planting layers of trees, shrubs, herbs, and ground covers that work together to promote soil health, water retention, and nutrient cycling.

Forest gardens can include layers such as:

Tall Fruit Trees (e.g., apple, pear, chestnut)

Smaller Trees and Shrubs (e.g., hazelnut, elderberry)

Herb Layer (e.g., rosemary, oregano)

Ground Cover (e.g., strawberries, clover)

Root Layer (e.g., garlic, onions)

By stacking plants vertically and including a wide variety of species, you maximize productivity while creating a more resilient system that requires fewer inputs like fertilizers and pesticides.

Planning for Water Management:

Proper water management is critical for perennial systems. Install swales and rainwater catchment systems to direct and store rainwater efficiently. Swales placed on contour lines around trees and berry bushes capture runoff and allow it to soak into the soil, providing moisture to plants during dry periods.

Mulching and ground covers also play essential roles in conserving moisture. Planting clover as a ground cover around fruit trees can help fix nitrogen in the soil while providing additional organic matter when it is mowed or breaks down naturally.

Creating a Year-Round Harvest Plan

Perennial plants offer the advantage of providing food at different times of the year. Planning your orchard and perennial beds for staggered harvests ensures that you have fresh produce throughout the growing season and beyond.

Staggered Harvesting of Fruit Trees:

Select fruit varieties that ripen at different times to extend the harvest period. For example, plant early-season apples (like Honeycrisp) alongside mid-season varieties (like Fuji) and late-season varieties (like Granny Smith). This approach prevents all your fruit from maturing simultaneously, reducing spoilage and spreading out processing tasks.

Berry bushes can also be staggered. Plant early-producing varieties like strawberries for spring harvests, followed by blueberries and blackberries in summer, and raspberries for fall.

Preserving and Storing Produce:

Plan for preserving fruit during peak harvest periods to ensure a year-round supply. Canning, drying, and freezing are effective methods for extending the life of fruit. For instance, apples can be turned into applesauce, dried into chips, or stored whole in cool, dry conditions for several months.

Berries can be frozen immediately after picking, or processed into jams and jellies. Invest in a dehydrator to make dried fruits, which are excellent for long-term storage and convenient off-grid snacking.

Adding Perennial Vegetables for Extended Harvests:

Beyond fruit trees and berries, perennial vegetables like asparagus, rhubarb, artichokes, and sorrel provide early-season harvests and continue producing for many years. These vegetables are hardy and require minimal care once established.

Incorporate perennial greens like kale, chard, and walking onions that can be harvested throughout the growing season, ensuring a continuous supply of fresh vegetables even when annual crops are out of season.

Integrating Fruit and Nut Trees with Livestock:

Utilizing orchards as dual-purpose areas for fruit production and grazing helps integrate livestock with your perennial systems. Animals such as chickens, goats, or sheep can be rotated through orchards to manage weeds and fertilize the soil naturally.

Grazing animals help keep grass and other growth under control, reducing competition for resources with the trees. Ensure that livestock is managed properly to prevent damage to young trees by using temporary fencing or tree guards.

Conclusion: Establishing a Resilient Perennial System

By planting fruit trees, berry bushes, and perennial vegetables, you create a long-term food supply that requires minimal replanting and supports a self-sustaining homestead. Combining these plants with sustainable practices such as companion planting, organic pest control, and crop diversity ensures that your orchard and perennial beds remain productive and resilient.

The next chapter will delve into water collection systems, focusing on how to gather and manage rainwater efficiently to support your garden, orchard, and livestock, ensuring a consistent water supply even in off-grid settings.

Chapter 9: Gathering Fresh Water: Rainwater Harvesting Systems

Water is one of the most critical resources for an off-grid homestead. Without a reliable source, it becomes challenging to maintain gardens, livestock, or even basic household needs. While wells and natural springs are excellent sources, rainwater harvesting provides an accessible and sustainable way to supplement water supplies, especially in areas with limited groundwater availability. This chapter covers the essentials of designing a rainwater catchment system, how to store and manage the collected water, and the legal considerations that homesteaders should be aware of.

Designing a Rainwater Catchment System for Homesteads

Setting up an efficient rainwater harvesting system involves capturing rainwater from rooftops and directing it into storage tanks for future use. The key components include a catchment surface (typically the roof), gutters, downspouts, filters, and storage tanks.

Selecting a Suitable Catchment Surface:

The roof of your home or barn is the most practical surface for capturing rainwater. Metal roofs are ideal as they are smooth, durable, and easy to clean. They also do not leach harmful chemicals into the water, unlike some asphalt shingles or treated wood.

Make sure the catchment surface is free from contaminants, such as bird droppings, debris, or chemical residues. Regularly inspect and clean the roof to ensure that it remains a safe source for collecting water.

Gutters and Downspouts:

Gutters and downspouts are essential for directing rainwater from the roof to your storage tanks. Install gutters along the roof edges, ensuring they have a slight slope (about 1/16 inch per foot) to direct water flow efficiently toward the downspouts.

Downspouts should be connected to a first flush diverter, which is a device that prevents the first few gallons of rainfall from entering the storage tanks. This initial water often carries debris and contaminants from the roof. Once the first flush is diverted, clean water flows into the storage tanks.

Consider adding gutter guards or mesh screens to prevent leaves, twigs, and other debris from entering the system. Keeping the gutters clear ensures efficient water flow and reduces maintenance needs.

Storage Tanks and Capacity Planning:

Rainwater storage tanks come in various sizes and materials, including plastic, fiberglass, and metal. The size of the tank depends on your rainfall patterns, roof surface area, and water needs. For example, a 1,000-square-foot roof can collect approximately 600 gallons of water per inch of rainfall.

To calculate the tank size you need, estimate your monthly water usage (for garden irrigation, household use, and livestock) and match it with your area's average monthly rainfall. It's often beneficial to install multiple smaller tanks instead of one large one, as this provides flexibility and redundancy.

Place tanks on elevated stands or platforms to allow gravity-fed systems for garden irrigation and household use. Ensure the tanks are secured and protected from UV light, which can degrade the material over time and promote algae growth.

Storing and Managing Rainwater for Household and Garden Use

Once your rainwater harvesting system is set up, it's important to manage and use the water efficiently. Proper storage, filtration, and distribution methods ensure that the water remains safe and accessible for various purposes.

Filtration Systems:

Rainwater collected directly from rooftops may contain debris, bacteria, or chemicals, so filtering it before use is crucial. A basic filtration system should include a coarse filter at the tank inlet to capture large particles and a fine filter before water is distributed to the house or garden.

For household use, especially for drinking and cooking, installing a multi-stage filtration system is recommended. This typically includes:

Sediment Filters: Remove sand, dirt, and small debris.

Carbon Filters: Eliminate organic compounds, chlorine, and unpleasant odors.

UV Sterilizers: Kill bacteria and viruses, ensuring the water is safe for consumption.

Regularly maintain and replace filters to prevent clogging and ensure water quality.

Gravity-Fed vs. Pump Systems:

Gravity-fed systems are an effective way to deliver water to gardens or household taps without the need for electricity. By placing storage tanks at an elevated height, you can use gravity to generate sufficient water pressure for most uses, such as drip irrigation or simple outdoor taps.

For more advanced systems, especially those providing water inside the house, a pressure pump may be needed to maintain consistent water pressure. Solar-powered pumps are an excellent option for off-grid homesteads, offering reliability without relying on grid electricity.

Water Storage and Treatment:

Storing rainwater properly is essential to maintain its quality. Tanks should be covered to prevent contamination from insects, rodents, or sunlight. UV exposure promotes algae growth, so use opaque tanks or place them in shaded areas to minimize this risk.

For potable water, adding a small amount of food-grade chlorine or using UV purification systems can help maintain water safety. It's important to monitor and test water regularly to ensure it meets safe drinking standards, especially during dry periods when water levels may be low and contamination risks higher.

Managing Water for Garden Irrigation:

Rainwater is naturally soft and free of chemicals like chlorine, making it ideal for garden use. Integrate the rainwater storage system with drip irrigation or soaker hoses to minimize evaporation and deliver water directly to plant roots. This method conserves water and promotes healthy growth, as plants receive a consistent supply of moisture.

Incorporate rain gardens or swales around your property to maximize rainwater use. Swales are shallow ditches that capture and slowly release water into the soil, helping to irrigate nearby plants naturally. Rain gardens can be planted with moisture-loving plants and serve as a natural filtration system for runoff water, improving overall soil health.

Winterizing the System:

In colder climates, winterizing your rainwater system is necessary to prevent damage. Drain and disconnect hoses, and use insulation wraps for pipes and tanks to prevent freezing. Some homesteaders opt for buried tanks that are insulated by the earth, which keeps water at a stable temperature year-round.

Alternatively, collecting and storing rainwater in smaller, portable tanks that can be moved to protected areas during winter months is another way to avoid freeze damage while keeping some water available for essential use.

Legal Considerations for Rainwater Harvesting

While rainwater harvesting is a sustainable and practical solution, it is not universally allowed or regulated the same way across all regions. Understanding the legal considerations and restrictions in your area is essential to avoid fines or conflicts.

State and Local Regulations:

In some regions, rainwater collection is restricted or regulated due to water rights laws. States like Colorado and Utah have historically placed limits on the volume of rainwater that can be collected, based on the belief that capturing rainwater reduces runoff that would otherwise replenish groundwater and streams. However, many of these laws have been updated or relaxed in recent years, so it's important to check the current regulations in your area.

Some areas may require permits for installing large storage tanks or using rainwater for certain purposes (such as potable water). Contact your local water authority or planning department to learn about any requirements or permits necessary for your system.

Water Rights and Usage Restrictions:

In regions where water rights are tightly controlled, rainwater collection may be limited to non-potable uses only, such as garden irrigation or car washing. In these cases, it's essential to keep your potable and non-potable water systems separate and properly labeled to comply with regulations.

If you live in an area with strict regulations, work with local authorities to design a compliant system. For example, demonstrating how your system uses overflow channels or integrates rain gardens to return water to the natural environment may help gain approval for larger collection systems.

Building Codes and Zoning Laws:

Installing rainwater tanks and catchment systems may also be subject to building codes and zoning laws. For example, large tanks may need to be anchored properly and adhere to setback requirements from property lines or structures.

Roof modifications, such as installing gutter systems or adjusting downspouts, might require a building permit. To avoid any issues, consult your local building department before starting construction, and use approved materials that meet regional building codes.

Environmental Considerations and Best Practices

While designing and implementing a rainwater harvesting system, it is crucial to consider the broader environmental impact. Best practices not only help maintain legal compliance but also ensure that your system supports the natural ecosystem around your homestead.

Maintaining Natural Water Flow:

Diverting too much water from natural pathways can disrupt local ecosystems. When designing your system, ensure that overflow from storage tanks or first flush diverters returns to the environment in a controlled manner, such as through rain gardens or percolation pits that slowly release water back into the soil.

Avoid disrupting natural streams or drainage patterns when setting up catchment systems. Keeping the water flow as close to its natural state as possible prevents erosion and supports local wildlife.

Using Eco-Friendly Materials:

Choose non-toxic materials for gutters, downspouts, and storage tanks. PVC and food-grade polyethylene are popular choices, but ensure they are UV-resistant and free from harmful chemicals that could leach into the water.

For eco-friendly filtration, opt for natural charcoal or sand filters, which are biodegradable and less harmful to dispose of compared to some synthetic options.

Integrating with Other Water Systems:

Combining rainwater harvesting with greywater recycling enhances water conservation efforts. Greywater, which comes from sources like sinks, showers, and washing machines, can be treated and used for irrigation. Connecting both systems provides a more comprehensive water management approach, reducing the homestead's reliance on other water sources.

Use rainwater to supplement existing well or spring systems during dry periods. By integrating different water sources, you create a more resilient system capable of withstanding seasonal changes or unexpected water shortages.

Scaling and Upgrading Your Rainwater Harvesting System

For many homesteaders, starting with a basic rainwater system and expanding over time is a practical approach. As you assess your water needs and usage patterns, scaling the system ensures it remains efficient and meets your requirements.

Adding Additional Storage Tanks:

If you find that your initial storage capacity is insufficient, adding additional tanks is a straightforward solution. Link tanks using interconnected pipes to balance water levels between them automatically. This method increases capacity without needing to replace the existing system.

Consider installing tanks of different sizes and placing them strategically around the property. Smaller tanks can be dedicated to garden areas, while larger ones may be used for household use or livestock.

Implementing Advanced Filtration and Monitoring:

Upgrading your filtration system is important if you plan to use rainwater for potable purposes. Adding multi-stage filters and UV sterilizers ensures the water remains safe and free from contaminants. Monitor water quality regularly using test kits or connect your system to smart sensors that track levels of turbidity, pH, and bacterial presence.

A rainwater monitoring system can also provide real-time data on water levels and usage, helping you manage the resource more efficiently. Automated controls can divert water to different tanks or initiate irrigation based on moisture levels in the garden, maximizing efficiency.

Optimizing the System for Long-Term Sustainability

Ensuring the longevity and sustainability of your rainwater system involves regular maintenance and adjustments based on environmental and seasonal changes.

Regular System Inspections:

Inspect gutters, downspouts, and tanks regularly for debris buildup or damage. Clean gutters at least twice a year, especially before and after the rainy season, to maintain efficient water flow. Check for leaks in the system and repair them promptly to prevent water loss.

Test the efficiency of the filtration system by monitoring water clarity and performing water quality tests. Replace filters as needed and ensure UV systems are functioning correctly.

Adapting to Seasonal Changes:

In regions with distinct wet and dry seasons, plan for varying water availability. During rainy periods, ensure tanks are prepared to handle overflow, directing excess water to swales or rain gardens. In drier months, monitor usage carefully to prevent depletion.

Adjust the catchment system based on weather forecasts. For example, during heavy storms, temporarily disconnect downspouts if tanks are full to prevent overflow damage. On the other hand, during prolonged dry spells, ration water carefully for essential uses like livestock and vegetable gardens.

Future-Proofing with Alternative Water Sources:

Rainwater harvesting systems are highly effective, but they should be integrated with other water sources like wells or ponds for redundancy. In case of drought or unexpected maintenance needs, having multiple water supplies ensures your homestead remains functional.

Building ponds or cisterns on your property can supplement rainwater storage and provide habitat for fish or irrigation options during dry periods. Using solar-powered pumps to circulate water from these sources into the main storage tanks can reduce dependence on a single water source.

Benefits of Rainwater Harvesting for Off-Grid Living

Rainwater harvesting offers numerous benefits beyond simply providing a water source. It's a sustainable practice that reduces reliance on wells, municipal supplies, and other non-renewable water sources. Additionally, rainwater is naturally soft and free from chemicals like chlorine, making it ideal for gardens and livestock.

Lower Environmental Impact:

By capturing and using rainwater, you reduce runoff, which can lead to erosion and pollution in local waterways. Properly designed systems help manage water on-site, improving soil health and supporting local wildlife.

Reducing the strain on groundwater resources is another advantage. In areas where groundwater levels are declining, rainwater systems are a sustainable alternative that supports long-term water availability.

Cost-Effective and Flexible:

Rainwater harvesting systems can be scaled according to your budget. Simple systems start with a few hundred dollars for basic tanks and gutters, while more complex setups with advanced filtration can be added over time as resources allow.

Once installed, rainwater systems have low operating costs, relying on gravity or solar pumps to distribute water, making them ideal for off-grid homesteads looking to reduce utility expenses.

Conclusion: Building a Reliable Rainwater Harvesting System

Rainwater harvesting is an essential component of an off-grid homestead, providing a sustainable and flexible water source for gardens, livestock, and household needs. By designing an efficient catchment system, ensuring proper filtration, and understanding the legal and environmental considerations, you can establish a reliable water supply that supports your off-grid lifestyle.

In the next chapter, we'll explore waste management solutions, focusing on how to create composting toilets and greywater systems that recycle resources and support a sustainable, self-sufficient homestead.

Chapter 10: Finding and Collecting Groundwater

Groundwater is a vital resource for off-grid homesteads, providing a consistent and reliable water supply when surface water sources like rivers or rainwater collection systems may be insufficient. Locating and accessing natural groundwater sources such as wells, springs, and rivers is an essential skill for off-grid living. In this chapter, we'll cover how to identify and develop these sources, including constructing and maintaining wells, and ensuring groundwater safety through proper sanitation and precautions.

Locating Natural Water Sources: Wells, Springs, and Rivers

Identifying natural water sources on or near your property is the first step in developing a reliable off-grid water supply. Understanding the terrain, soil composition, and signs of groundwater presence can help you make informed decisions about where and how to access this critical resource.

Identifying Springs:

Springs are natural outflows of groundwater that emerge at the surface. They often occur in areas where the water table intersects with the earth's surface, typically in valleys or hillsides. Signs of a spring include lush vegetation, damp ground, or visible pools of water, even during dry periods.

Springs provide a direct source of fresh water that may require minimal intervention beyond ensuring it remains clean. If you locate a spring on your property, observe it over several seasons to confirm that it flows consistently throughout the year before relying on it as your primary water source.

Rivers and Streams:

Rivers and streams are surface water sources that can be utilized for irrigation, livestock watering, or filtration for household use. However, their flow is often seasonal and dependent on rainfall patterns. For homesteads close to reliable streams, installing pumps or building small dams can be useful for channeling water into storage tanks.

Before using river or stream water, consider its quality and potential contaminants. Surface water can contain pathogens, chemicals from upstream activities, or sediment, all of which require filtration and purification for safe use.

Drilling Wells:

Wells provide direct access to groundwater stored in underground aquifers. Drilling a well is an effective way to secure a steady water supply, particularly in areas where surface water or rain collection is insufficient. Locating the best spot for drilling involves surveying the land and consulting geological maps that indicate aquifer depths and locations.

Working with a professional hydrologist or water diviner (dowser) can help identify the most promising areas for drilling. Geological features such as valleys, riverbeds, or depressions are often good indicators of accessible groundwater, as they naturally collect water from surrounding areas.

Constructing a Well: Equipment, Setup, and Maintenance

Constructing a well involves significant planning and the right equipment. Whether you plan to hire professionals or undertake the project yourself, understanding the process is crucial for ensuring the well is safe, efficient, and long-lasting.

Types of Wells:

Dug Wells: These are traditional wells, often excavated by hand or with machinery. They are relatively shallow (typically 10-30 feet deep) and rely on groundwater close to the surface. Dug wells are suitable for areas with a high water table but are more susceptible to contamination.

Driven Wells: These wells are created by driving a pipe into the ground using a well-point and are usually shallow (up to 50 feet). They are relatively easy to install but are also vulnerable to contamination if not properly sealed.

Drilled Wells: The most reliable and long-lasting option, drilled wells can reach depths of several hundred feet, accessing deeper aquifers. These wells require professional drilling rigs and are typically more expensive but provide cleaner, more consistent water supplies.

Equipment Needed for Well Construction:

Drilling Rig: For deeper wells, a drilling rig is necessary to penetrate bedrock and reach the aquifer. Small-scale homesteaders can rent rigs or hire drilling services to complete this part of the process. Auger-based systems are an option for shallower wells.

Casing: The well casing is a pipe inserted into the drilled hole to prevent it from collapsing and to protect the water source from contaminants. Casings are usually made of PVC or steel and extend from the surface down to the aquifer. Properly installed casings are crucial for maintaining water quality and structural stability.

Pump Systems: Pumps are necessary to bring water from the well to the surface. Hand pumps are effective for shallow wells and do not require electricity, while submersible electric pumps are used for deeper wells. For off-grid homesteads, solar-powered pumps offer an efficient and sustainable option.

Well Drilling Process:

Once the location is identified, begin by drilling the borehole. This process can take several days, depending on the depth and ground conditions. Ensure the borehole remains straight, as misalignment can cause issues with casing installation and water retrieval.

After reaching the aquifer, install the well casing, ensuring it is securely seated and extends above ground level to prevent surface water from entering. Seal the area around the casing with grout or bentonite clay to create a sanitary seal, which is essential for preventing contaminants from reaching the water source.

Install the pump system and connect it to the power source. Test the pump to verify that it is drawing water efficiently and without contamination.

Well Maintenance Essentials:

Maintaining a well involves regular inspections to ensure the casing and pump remain in good condition. Inspect the well cap, which should be tightly sealed to prevent animals, insects, or surface water from entering the system.

Test the water quality periodically (at least annually) to check for contaminants like bacteria, nitrates, or chemicals. Maintaining proper records of water quality helps identify any emerging issues early, allowing you to take corrective action before problems escalate.

For homesteads using electric pumps, ensure that the solar panels (if applicable) or other power sources remain functional and clean. Replace filters and inspect wiring connections to maintain consistent water flow.

Safety Precautions and Sanitation for Groundwater Use

Groundwater can be a reliable source of fresh water, but it must be managed carefully to ensure safety and prevent contamination. Proper sanitation practices are crucial for maintaining water quality and ensuring the well remains a safe and sustainable resource.

Ensuring Safe Well Water:

Groundwater can be contaminated by agricultural runoff, septic systems, and natural pollutants like heavy metals. Regular testing for E. coli, coliform bacteria, and chemical contaminants is essential, especially after heavy rains or flooding events, which can carry contaminants into the groundwater.

Installing a UV water purifier or a chlorination system can help disinfect water and eliminate harmful pathogens. Additionally, using a carbon filter can remove organic chemicals and improve water taste and clarity.

Preventing Contamination:

To protect your well from contamination, keep any potential sources of pollution, such as livestock pens, septic systems, or chemical storage, at least 100 feet away from the well. This separation reduces the risk of contaminants seeping into the water source.

Maintain the area around the well clean and free from debris or standing water. Vegetative buffers, like grass or low shrubs, can help absorb runoff and filter potential contaminants before they reach the well site.

Proper Sealing and Casing Installation:

A well-sealed casing is critical for maintaining the integrity of the water source. Ensure that the casing is securely anchored and extends well above ground level to prevent surface water from flowing directly into the well.

If you notice any cracks or damage to the casing, repair it promptly. Small leaks can allow contaminants to enter the well and compromise water quality. Use bentonite clay or cement to reseal any gaps around the casing to maintain a tight barrier.

Water Treatment Systems:

For deeper wells that may draw from aquifers containing minerals like iron or manganese, installing a water softener can help manage these elements. Iron filters can also prevent staining of household fixtures and ensure water remains clear.

Advanced filtration systems, such as reverse osmosis, are effective for removing a broad spectrum of contaminants, including heavy metals and chemicals. While these systems require maintenance and energy, they provide an added level of protection, particularly if you plan to use well water for drinking.

Sanitation Protocols for Well Construction and Maintenance

Constructing and maintaining a well involves handling soil and water, which can introduce contaminants if proper hygiene practices are not followed. Implementing sanitation protocols minimizes risks during well installation and ongoing management.

Sanitary Construction Practices:

During well construction, ensure that the borehole, casing, and surrounding area are kept clean. Workers should wash hands and tools frequently and avoid contaminating the site with external sources like dirty footwear or unclean equipment.

Use sanitized tools for installing the pump and any filtration systems. Well casings and other components should be cleaned and disinfected before installation to reduce the introduction of pathogens into the well.

Post-Construction Well Disinfection:

Once a well is constructed, it should be disinfected to eliminate any bacteria introduced during drilling. A common method is to add chlorine bleach (following the correct concentration guidelines) and circulate it through the system. After allowing the chlorine to sit for several hours, flush the well until the water is clear and free from chlorine odor.

Test the water again after disinfection to ensure that it meets safe drinking standards. Continue testing periodically, especially after heavy rains or other events that could impact groundwater levels.

Best Practices for Ongoing Well Management

Maintaining well water quality and ensuring long-term reliability involves proactive management and adherence to best practices.

Monitoring Water Levels:

For homesteads relying heavily on well water, monitoring the water level regularly helps track seasonal fluctuations and predict shortages. Installing a water level gauge allows you to keep an eye on groundwater levels and adjust usage as needed to prevent over-extraction.

In areas prone to drought, conserve water by limiting non-essential uses and supplementing with alternative water sources like rainwater harvesting during peak dry seasons.

Protecting the Water Table:

Overuse of groundwater can lower the water table, affecting not only your well but also surrounding wells and natural springs. Practicing rotational water use by alternating between rainwater and well water can help preserve the aquifer.

Planting native vegetation around the homestead that is adapted to the local climate reduces the need for excessive watering. Mulching gardens and using efficient irrigation methods, like drip systems, also help minimize water use.

Dealing with Seasonal Variations and Drought:

During drought conditions, well water may become more scarce. It's important to prepare by installing additional storage tanks that can be filled when water levels are high. This reserves water for drier periods and maintains a buffer supply.

If water levels drop significantly, consider deepening the well or drilling an additional one in another location on the property to diversify access points. Ensure that these measures comply with local regulations and are designed to minimize long-term environmental impact.

Ensuring Groundwater Safety and Reliability

For off-grid homesteaders, keeping groundwater safe and reliable is a continuous process involving both technical maintenance and sustainable practices.

Seasonal Maintenance Checks:

Conduct thorough well inspections before and after extreme weather seasons, such as winter and the rainy season. Check for any structural damage or water quality changes that may occur due to freezing, heavy rains, or other natural events.

Test pump efficiency regularly and inspect electrical connections, especially for solar-powered or electric pump systems, to ensure that everything functions optimally.

Sustainable Water Practices:

Combining groundwater use with other water sources like rainwater harvesting and greywater recycling not only preserves the aquifer but also creates a more resilient water system. Design your homestead's water infrastructure to accommodate multiple inputs, allowing for seamless transition between sources as needed.

Emergency Measures and Backup Plans

Preparing for emergencies is an essential aspect of off-grid well management. Whether it's a pump failure, contamination, or natural disaster, having contingency plans ensures that your water supply remains secure.

Installing Backup Pump Systems:

For deeper wells, keeping a manual hand pump as a backup ensures access to water if electric or solar-powered pumps fail. Install a hand pump in parallel with the electric system so that it can be activated quickly during power outages.

In areas with unreliable solar exposure, include a backup generator capable of powering the pump system. Diesel or propane generators are common off-grid options that provide flexibility when solar energy is insufficient.

Contingency Planning for Contamination Events:

If the well becomes contaminated due to natural disasters like flooding or chemical spills, having a secondary source of water is critical. Rainwater tanks and portable filtration systems, such as gravity-fed ceramic filters, can provide safe drinking water until the well is decontaminated.

Establish an emergency plan for well shutdown, including sealing the well cap and stopping water usage until testing confirms the water is safe. Keep a stock of purification tablets, water barrels, and emergency supplies to ensure continued access to potable water.

Conclusion: Accessing and Managing Groundwater Safely

Groundwater is a crucial resource for any off-grid homestead, providing a steady supply of water for drinking, irrigation, and livestock. By locating natural water sources, constructing and maintaining wells properly, and adhering to sanitation protocols, you can ensure that your homestead has a safe and sustainable water supply. Combining groundwater use with other methods like rainwater harvesting and water conservation practices creates a resilient system capable of meeting your homestead's needs year-round.

In the next chapter, we'll explore off-grid waste management solutions, focusing on composting toilets, greywater systems, and safe disposal practices that support a sustainable and environmentally friendly homestead.

Chapter 11: Water Purification Techniques

Access to clean, safe water is a fundamental need for any off-grid homestead. Whether you source your water from a well, river, rainwater collection system, or natural spring, purification is often necessary to eliminate contaminants and ensure the water is safe for drinking and cooking. This chapter covers various water purification methods, from filtration and boiling to chemical treatments. We'll also discuss how to build a DIY water filter using natural materials and outline best practices for storing purified water safely for long-term use.

Methods for Purifying Water: Filtration, Boiling, and Chemical Treatment

Effective water purification typically involves multiple steps to remove particles, bacteria, viruses, and chemical contaminants. Depending on your water source and available resources, you may need to combine several methods for the best results.

Filtration: Removing Sediment and Particles

Filtration is the first step in purifying water and involves passing it through a medium that removes sediment, debris, and microorganisms. Commercial filters such as ceramic, carbon, or sand filters are widely used and effective for off-grid setups.

Ceramic Filters: These have tiny pores that physically block bacteria and parasites while allowing water to pass through. Some ceramic filters also have silver embedded in them, which acts as a bactericide. Ceramic filters are durable and reusable with proper cleaning, making them ideal for long-term use.

Carbon Filters: Activated carbon filters are effective for removing organic compounds, chlorine, and unpleasant tastes and odors. While they don't eliminate viruses, they improve the taste of water and reduce chemical contaminants.

Sand Filters: A simple and efficient option, sand filters use layers of sand and gravel to trap particles. They are particularly useful for treating river or rainwater but need regular cleaning and maintenance to stay effective.

Boiling: The Most Reliable Method

Boiling water is one of the simplest and most reliable ways to kill harmful microorganisms, including bacteria, viruses, and parasites. To ensure water is safe, bring it to a rolling boil for at least 1 minute; if you are at higher altitudes (above 6,500 feet), boil for at least 3 minutes to account for lower boiling temperatures.

Boiling is an excellent method for emergency purification but requires a consistent energy source (e.g., wood, propane, or solar cooker). While effective, boiling alone does not remove sediment or chemical contaminants, so it should be combined with filtration if these are present.

Chemical Treatment: Using Chlorine or Iodine

Chemical disinfectants like chlorine (household bleach) and iodine tablets are effective in killing bacteria, viruses, and most protozoa. However, they do not remove sediment or improve the taste of water, so they are often used in combination with filtration methods.

Chlorine Treatment: Use unscented household bleach (sodium hypochlorite) that contains no additives. Add 8 drops per gallon of clear water or 16 drops per gallon if the water is cloudy. Stir well and let the water stand for at least 30 minutes before use. If you can smell a slight chlorine odor after treatment, the water is safe to drink; if not, repeat the process.

Iodine Treatment: Iodine tablets are convenient and effective for short-term or emergency use. Add the recommended number of tablets per liter, shake well, and let the water sit for at least 30 minutes before consumption. Note that prolonged use of iodine is not recommended for pregnant women or individuals with thyroid issues.

UV Purification: Portable and Effective

UV light purifiers are another effective option, particularly for off-grid homesteads using solar power. UV purifiers use ultraviolet light to kill microorganisms by disrupting their DNA. Handheld UV devices are portable and easy to use; simply stir the UV wand in a liter of clear water for the recommended time (usually about 90 seconds).

This method works well for clear water but may be less effective for murky or sediment-laden water, as UV light cannot penetrate particles. Filtering the water first is crucial for maximum effectiveness.

DIY Water Filter Construction Using Natural Materials

Building a water filter from natural materials is a practical solution for off-grid homesteaders, especially in emergency situations or remote areas where commercial filters may not be available. Here's how to create a simple yet effective water filter using materials like sand, gravel, charcoal, and cloth.

Materials Needed:

A container (like a plastic bottle or large PVC pipe)

Sand and gravel (in different sizes)

Charcoal (activated charcoal is best, but you can also use charcoal from a fire)

Cloth or a piece of mesh for layering

Stones or pebbles for the top layer

Layering the Filter:

Cut the bottom off the container and invert it so the open end is facing down. This will serve as the base where water will flow out.

Layer 1: Place a cloth or mesh layer at the bottom to act as the first filtration barrier. This prevents sand and charcoal from washing out.

Layer 2: Add a layer of fine sand (2-3 inches thick). Sand traps smaller particles and helps clarify the water.

Layer 3: Add a layer of activated charcoal (about 2 inches). The charcoal absorbs organic compounds, improves taste, and removes odors.

Layer 4: Add a layer of coarse sand (2 inches) and then a layer of small gravel (2-3 inches) on top of that. These layers trap larger particles and debris, further clarifying the water.

Layer 5: Place a top layer of larger stones or pebbles. This acts as the initial filter for the water and keeps the smaller layers beneath intact.

Using the Filter:

Pour water slowly into the top of the filter and allow it to pass through each layer. The filtered water will collect at the bottom, where it can be collected in a container. While this method removes particles and some pathogens, it is recommended to boil or treat the filtered water with chemicals (like chlorine) for complete purification.

Maintenance and Limitations:

A DIY filter requires regular maintenance. Rinse and replace the sand and gravel layers periodically, and refresh the charcoal every few weeks to maintain effectiveness. Ensure the filter remains upright and stable to prevent contamination.

This type of filter works best for sediment-laden or cloudy water but may not remove all bacteria and viruses. Combining it with another purification method like boiling or UV treatment is advised for drinking purposes.

Storing Purified Water Safely for Long-Term Use

Once water is purified, it's important to store it properly to maintain its safety and quality. Here are best practices for storing water for both short-term and long-term use.

Choosing the Right Containers:

Use food-grade containers made of materials such as BPA-free plastic, stainless steel, or glass. These containers are designed to prevent chemicals from leaching into the water, keeping it safe for consumption. Avoid using old milk jugs or any container that has previously stored non-food items, as they may harbor contaminants.

For long-term storage, opt for opaque containers that block light, as exposure to sunlight can promote algae growth and degrade water quality.

Storage Location and Conditions:

Store purified water in a cool, dark place, such as a pantry, basement, or root cellar. Avoid areas that are exposed to extreme temperatures, as heat and freezing conditions can damage containers and affect water quality.

Ensure that the storage area is clean and free of potential contaminants, such as chemicals or fumes, which can permeate plastic containers over time.

Water Rotation and Treatment:

Even purified water should be rotated periodically to ensure freshness. For long-term storage, rotate water every 6-12 months. Label containers with the date of purification to keep track of when they were filled.

If storing water for more than a year, consider adding a small amount of chlorine bleach (1/8 teaspoon per gallon) to maintain disinfection. This helps prevent bacterial growth, especially if the water has been exposed to air or light.

Emergency Storage Tips:

For emergency preparedness, maintain a supply of portable water containers that can be easily transported if needed. Collapsible containers or water bladders are excellent options for emergencies, as they are compact and easy to fill when necessary.

Keep a supply of water purification tablets on hand in case you need to purify stored water quickly. Tablets are easy to use and effective for small quantities, making them ideal for emergency kits.

Creating a Long-Term Water Storage System for Off-Grid Living

For homesteaders aiming for complete self-sufficiency, setting up a comprehensive water storage system ensures a steady supply of potable water throughout the year.

Designing a Water Storage Plan:

Calculate your daily water usage for drinking, cooking, and hygiene, and plan for at least one gallon per person per day as a minimum for emergency purposes. Multiply this amount by the number of days you want to be prepared for (e.g., 30 or 60 days) to determine your total storage needs.

Integrate your water storage with your collection systems (e.g., rainwater tanks or well storage) to maintain a seamless flow between sourcing, purifying, and storing water. This setup ensures that your water supply is continually replenished and filtered, reducing the need for frequent manual intervention.

Installing Large-Scale Storage Tanks:

For long-term solutions, install cisterns or large above-ground storage tanks that can hold hundreds or even thousands of gallons. These tanks are connected to rainwater or well systems and are often equipped with filtration units at the intake and outflow points.

Buried cisterns are particularly useful for off-grid homesteads, as they keep water cool and protected from sunlight. Ensure these tanks are equipped with access points for regular cleaning and inspection.

Water Storage Maintenance and Monitoring

Keeping stored water safe over time requires consistent monitoring and maintenance.

Regular Testing and Treatment:

Periodically test the stored water for bacteria, pH levels, and chemical contaminants, especially if the storage system is connected to untreated sources like wells or rivers. Use portable testing kits designed for drinking water to conduct these tests quickly and efficiently.

Treat stored water with UV light, chlorine, or iodine if tests indicate contamination. A UV purifier can be integrated into the storage system to treat water before it is distributed to household taps.

Cleaning and Sanitizing Tanks:

Empty and clean tanks every 6-12 months to prevent buildup of algae, sediment, and bacteria. Use a mild bleach solution (1 part bleach to 9 parts water) to sanitize the tank, then rinse thoroughly before refilling.

Regularly inspect the tank's seals and pipes for any leaks or damage. Promptly address any issues to prevent contamination and water loss.

Innovative Off-Grid Water Purification Solutions

As off-grid technology advances, new methods for purifying and storing water have become accessible for homesteaders.

Solar Water Distillation:

Solar distillation uses the sun's energy to purify water through evaporation and condensation. Building a simple solar still involves placing contaminated water in a clear basin covered by a transparent lid. The water evaporates, leaving contaminants behind, and then condenses on the lid, dripping into a collection tray.

This method is effective for producing small amounts of pure water from brackish or contaminated sources. It works best in sunny climates and requires no electricity, making it a valuable addition to off-grid water purification strategies.

Bio-Sand Filters:

Bio-sand filters are advanced versions of traditional sand filters, incorporating a biological layer (called the schmutzdecke) that forms naturally over time. This layer contains beneficial bacteria that consume harmful microorganisms in the water, enhancing purification.

Constructed using layers of gravel, sand, and an outlet pipe, bio-sand filters are low-maintenance and can be built using locally available materials. They are ideal for treating larger quantities of water and can last for years with minimal upkeep.

Using Ceramic Water Purifiers:

Ceramic purifiers, which are often combined with silver or activated carbon, offer another low-energy solution for off-grid homesteads. These filters can be installed as countertop units or attached directly to water storage tanks.

The ceramic material removes pathogens and improves clarity, while carbon components filter chemicals. For added protection, some units incorporate silver ions, which have natural antibacterial properties.

Integrating Water Purification into Homestead Systems

For a fully integrated and resilient water system, homesteaders should plan for water purification as part of a larger water management strategy.

Combining Water Sources:

Connecting multiple water sources (e.g., rainwater, well, and river) to a centralized purification system creates redundancy and increases resilience. Using pumps, filtration, and storage tanks, you can automate water treatment to maintain a consistent supply without constant manual labor.

Install diversion valves that allow you to switch between sources easily based on availability and quality. This flexibility ensures that if one source becomes contaminated or runs dry, the system continues to operate efficiently.

Monitoring and Automation:

Incorporate smart sensors into your water storage and purification systems. These sensors monitor water levels, pressure, and quality, sending alerts when maintenance or adjustments are needed. Automated UV filters and pumps can be programmed to activate when water enters the system, simplifying the purification process.

Long-Term Planning and Adaptation:

Off-grid homesteaders should plan for scalability and future upgrades. Start with basic filtration and storage systems that can be expanded as your needs grow. As technology evolves, consider integrating new solutions like solar-powered water purification units or advanced bio-filtration methods that require minimal maintenance.

Planning for potential climate changes or periods of drought is also crucial. Diversify your water sources and build extra storage capacity to manage water shortages effectively. By integrating rainwater harvesting with groundwater use and efficient filtration, you create a resilient and adaptable system capable of meeting future challenges.

Conclusion: Ensuring Safe and Reliable Water Purification

Establishing an effective water purification system is essential for off-grid living. By combining filtration, boiling, chemical treatments, and innovative methods like solar distillation or bio-sand filters, homesteaders can create a comprehensive and adaptable water management system. Proper storage and consistent maintenance ensure that purified water remains safe for long-term use, providing peace of mind and self-sufficiency.

In the next chapter, we will explore off-grid waste management solutions, including composting toilets and greywater systems, to help reduce waste and recycle resources effectively.

Chapter 12: Selecting and Preparing Your Homestead Location

Choosing the right location for your off-grid homestead is one of the most critical decisions in establishing a sustainable, self-sufficient lifestyle. The terrain, climate, and available resources of your property will significantly impact your ability to build, farm, and live independently. This chapter guides you through the process of selecting the best location for your homestead, including assessing the terrain and resources, preparing the land, and navigating legal considerations such as zoning laws and building permits.

Assessing Terrain, Climate, and Resources for Building Your Off-Grid Home

When selecting a homestead location, you must evaluate several key factors to ensure the site is suitable for your needs and goals. The terrain, local climate, and natural resources available on the land will all play important roles in determining how you design and manage your off-grid property.

Evaluating Terrain and Topography:

A site's terrain greatly affects where and how you can build structures, grow food, and manage water resources. Look for land with moderate slopes or flat areas, which are ideal for building and farming. Steep slopes may present challenges for construction and access but can be utilized for other purposes like grazing livestock or installing micro-hydro systems if you have a water source.

Pay attention to elevation as well. Higher elevations can offer cooler temperatures and better views but may also come with harsher weather conditions, shorter growing seasons, and less accessible roads.

Assessing Soil Quality and Vegetation:

Soil quality is essential for off-grid homesteaders who plan to grow food. Test the soil's pH and nutrient content using a soil testing kit or send samples to a local extension service. Ideal soil should have a balanced pH (between 6 and 7 for most crops) and adequate organic matter. Avoid land with heavy clay soils or soils that are too sandy, as these may require extensive amendments to become productive.

Vegetation on the land can also provide clues about soil quality and water availability. Healthy forests, native grasses, and lush vegetation often indicate fertile soil and access to water. However, areas with scrub brush or invasive species may require more work to clear and improve the soil for farming.

Climate and Weather Patterns:

Understanding the climate of your chosen location is vital for planning construction, gardening, and livestock management. Research the USDA Hardiness Zone or equivalent climate zone to understand which crops can thrive and the length of your growing season.

Investigate local weather patterns, such as rainfall and seasonal temperatures, to plan for water collection systems, insulation needs for buildings, and strategies for protecting crops from extreme weather. For example, areas with frequent droughts will benefit from rainwater harvesting systems and drought-resistant plants, while locations with cold winters require homes that can withstand snow loads and freezing temperatures.

Proximity to Natural Resources:

An ideal homestead location provides access to natural resources such as timber, stone, and water sources. These resources reduce the need for external materials and help you build and sustain your homestead independently. Timber can be used for building structures and fuel, while stone provides a durable material for foundations or pathways.

Water sources like rivers, streams, springs, or aquifers are crucial for providing a steady supply of water for household use, irrigation, and livestock. Sites without natural water sources can still be viable if there is sufficient rainfall for collection systems or if drilling a well is feasible.

Accessibility and Distance from Civilization:

While off-grid living often involves remote locations, accessibility remains important for transporting materials, accessing emergency services, and maintaining connections for supplies you cannot produce yourself. Evaluate the distance to the nearest town, the condition of roads, and whether they are passable year-round.

If the location is extremely remote, consider how you will manage transportation, such as using four-wheel-drive vehicles, snowmobiles, or even all-terrain vehicles (ATVs). These may be necessary for accessing your property during harsh weather conditions or for moving heavy materials during construction.

Clearing Land and Preparing the Foundation

Once you have chosen and purchased a suitable property, the next steps involve clearing the land and preparing the foundation for building your off-grid home. Proper planning and preparation are crucial to minimize environmental impact and ensure the foundation is stable.

Clearing the Land:

Start by creating a site plan that includes where structures, gardens, and other homestead features will be located. Clearing only the necessary areas helps preserve natural habitats and vegetation that can provide windbreaks, shade, or wildlife habitats.

Manual Clearing: In small areas or for light brush, manual clearing using hand tools like machetes, saws, or axes may be sufficient. This method allows for precise control and minimizes disturbance to the land but is labor-intensive.

Mechanical Clearing: For larger plots, renting machinery like tractors, chainsaws, or a brush hog can speed up the process. When using machinery, be mindful of soil erosion; avoid clearing during rainy seasons to prevent destabilizing the soil. Retain some vegetation to act as natural erosion control.

Establishing Access Points and Driveways:

Before building, ensure that there are access roads or driveways for bringing in materials. Gravel or dirt roads are common choices for off-grid properties, but they require grading and drainage systems to prevent erosion and maintain durability.

Avoid low-lying areas that may become waterlogged or difficult to traverse. Use local stone or gravel to reinforce roadways, ensuring they remain passable during adverse weather.

Laying the Foundation:

The foundation is one of the most critical aspects of building your off-grid home. Choose a foundation type that suits the terrain and climate of your property. Options include:

Concrete Slabs: Ideal for flat, stable ground, concrete slabs provide a solid base and can be insulated for colder climates. They are durable but require heavy equipment and materials, which may be challenging to access in remote areas.

Pier and Beam Foundations: These foundations are raised above ground on piers, making them suitable for uneven or sloped terrain. They provide natural ventilation under the house, helping with moisture control and insulation.

Stone Foundations: If local stone is available, a stone foundation offers a sustainable and long-lasting option. Stone foundations require skilled craftsmanship but blend well with the environment and can be built with minimal external materials.

Excavation and Site Preparation:

Excavation involves removing topsoil and leveling the site to create a stable area for the foundation. On sloped land, terracing or benching (creating flat steps) may be necessary to stabilize the ground and prevent erosion.

Install drainage systems around the foundation to manage water flow and reduce the risk of water damage. Swales, French drains, or retaining walls can direct water away from structures and help maintain soil stability.

Zoning Laws and Building Permits for Wilderness Properties

Building an off-grid home often involves navigating local zoning laws and obtaining building permits, even for remote or wilderness properties. These regulations are designed to ensure safety, environmental protection, and compliance with regional development plans.

Understanding Zoning Regulations:

Zoning laws dictate how land can be used, including whether it is designated for agricultural, residential, commercial, or mixed-use purposes. It is important to confirm that your intended use (e.g., building a residence and farming) aligns with the zoning classification of the property.

In rural areas, some land may be zoned as agricultural or wilderness with specific restrictions on building types, the number of structures allowed, and what activities can take place on the land. Consult local authorities to ensure that you are in compliance and to understand any requirements for agricultural or residential buildings.

Acquiring Building Permits:

Even for off-grid and wilderness properties, building permits are often required. These permits ensure that structures meet safety and environmental standards, including building codes for foundations, framing, plumbing, and electrical systems. Failure to obtain the proper permits can result in fines or the forced removal of structures.

Permit requirements vary by location, so it is essential to check with the county planning and zoning office or building department before beginning construction. Some areas have streamlined processes for small structures or agricultural buildings, but it's always better to verify what permits are necessary.

Permit Applications and Inspections:

The permit application process usually involves submitting detailed site plans and building blueprints that outline the intended construction and layout. You may need to provide additional information, such as water and sewage management plans (e.g., septic systems or composting toilets) and energy systems (e.g., solar installations).

Once a permit is approved, building inspectors may conduct site visits at different stages of construction to verify compliance with building codes. These inspections often cover foundation work, framing, electrical systems, and plumbing installations. It is crucial to schedule these inspections as needed and address any issues raised by inspectors promptly.

Managing Environmental Impact and Conservation Easements:

Many wilderness properties have environmental protection regulations in place to preserve local ecosystems, wildlife habitats, and water resources. Be aware of any conservation easements or protected areas on or near your property, which may restrict building or land-clearing activities.

Implementing sustainable practices, such as leaving buffer zones around streams or protecting forested areas, can help you comply with environmental laws. Building with local and natural materials (e.g., timber, stone) and minimizing disturbance to the landscape are also strategies that support sustainable development.

Legal Considerations and Property Rights

Ensuring you have a clear understanding of property rights and any legal obligations is vital before investing in a homestead location.

Surveying and Property Boundaries:

Conduct a thorough property survey to confirm the boundaries and dimensions of your land. This step helps avoid disputes with neighboring landowners and ensures that any structures built are within your property lines. Professional surveyors can provide detailed maps and documentation needed for permits and legal records.

Verify that there are no easements or rights of way across your property that could impact your plans. Easements allow others access to a portion of your land for purposes such as utilities, roads, or water rights, which may affect where you can build.

Water Rights and Access:

Water rights laws vary significantly by state and region. Before drilling a well or diverting water from a nearby stream or river, verify that you have the legal right to access and use that water source. In some areas, water rights are tied to land ownership, while in others, they must be separately acquired.

Ensure that your water management plans comply with state regulations to avoid legal issues. For instance, some states require permits for well drilling, and others have restrictions on the amount of water that can be collected or diverted for personal use.

Fire Safety and Prevention Regulations:

In wilderness areas, fire safety regulations are increasingly enforced due to the risk of wildfires. Many regions require defensible space around structures, which involves clearing vegetation, trees, and other potential fire fuels within a certain radius (often 100 feet).

Incorporate fire-resistant materials into your building plans and ensure that you have firebreaks and emergency water sources (e.g., water tanks or ponds) available for firefighting purposes. These measures are not only legal requirements but also vital for protecting your homestead in fire-prone areas.

Navigating Zoning Laws and Homesteader Rights

Understanding your rights as a homesteader and proactively working within legal frameworks can help you establish and develop your off-grid property without encountering roadblocks.

Applying for Zoning Variances:

If the zoning regulations do not align with your plans, applying for a zoning variance may be an option. Variances allow for exceptions to zoning laws under specific circumstances, such as building a small residential structure in an agricultural zone or constructing an eco-friendly dwelling.

To apply for a variance, you typically need to demonstrate that your project will not negatively impact the environment or surrounding properties. Working with local planners and attending zoning board meetings may be necessary to gain approval.

Seeking Legal Advice for Land Use and Development:

When navigating complex zoning laws, water rights issues, or building regulations, consulting with a real estate attorney who specializes in rural or agricultural properties can be beneficial. They can provide guidance on local laws and help you understand any long-term implications of your land use plans.

In some cases, forming a homesteader association with other local off-grid residents can provide a collective voice for advocating for more flexible zoning and building codes, promoting sustainable living practices.

Conclusion: Establishing a Secure and Legal Foundation for Your Homestead

Selecting and preparing a location for your off-grid homestead is a comprehensive process that requires careful planning and adherence to legal guidelines. By assessing terrain, climate, and resources, and understanding zoning laws and building permits, you can establish a secure foundation for your sustainable lifestyle. Proper preparation, including clearing land and building the right foundation, ensures that your homestead will thrive for years to come.

In the next chapter, we'll focus on building off-grid housing, covering the various construction methods and materials suitable for creating energy-efficient and sustainable homes.

Chapter 13: Off-Grid Housing: Shelter Types and Materials

Building a sustainable and efficient off-grid home is one of the most crucial steps in establishing a self-sufficient lifestyle. The right type of shelter provides not only protection from the elements but also comfort and energy efficiency. In this chapter, we explore various off-grid housing options, from cabins and tiny homes to earth-sheltered homes and yurts. We also discuss sustainable building materials and techniques for insulation and weatherproofing, ensuring that your off-grid home can withstand extreme climates and changing weather patterns.

Choosing the Right Type of Housing: Cabins, Tiny Homes, Earth-Sheltered Homes, and Yurts

The type of shelter you choose for your off-grid homestead will depend on factors such as climate, available materials, budget, and your specific needs. Each option offers unique benefits and challenges, making it important to carefully consider which design best suits your circumstances.

Cabins: Traditional and Reliable

Cabins are one of the most popular choices for off-grid living due to their simplicity and adaptability. They can be constructed using locally sourced timber, which reduces costs and environmental impact. Cabins are well-suited for colder climates as they offer the possibility of thick walls and insulation to retain heat.

Log Cabins: Using full logs provides natural insulation and a rustic aesthetic. Log cabins require skill in notching and stacking logs correctly to create a solid, weather-resistant structure. The main challenges involve managing moisture and preventing wood rot, so proper treatment and sealing are essential.

Framed Cabins: These are built using a wooden frame and are often quicker to construct than log cabins. Framed cabins offer flexibility for adding insulation materials between the studs, making them suitable for both hot and cold climates. They can be clad with wood siding, metal, or other durable materials depending on the aesthetic and functional preferences.

Tiny Homes: Efficient and Portable

Tiny homes have gained popularity in recent years as compact, efficient living spaces. They are ideal for those who prefer a minimalistic lifestyle and are often designed to be mobile, allowing for flexibility in location. Tiny homes are efficient to heat and cool, making them suitable for off-grid energy systems like solar panels.

Building a tiny home offers the advantage of needing fewer materials and less labor, which reduces costs. However, due to their small size, careful planning is required to maximize storage, insulation, and water management systems.

Earth-Sheltered Homes: Energy Efficient and Environmentally Integrated

Earth-sheltered homes, also known as earthships or underground homes, use the natural insulation properties of the earth to maintain stable indoor temperatures year-round. These homes are designed to be partially or fully buried into a hillside or covered with soil, making them highly energy efficient and suitable for extreme climates, especially cold or arid environments.

The construction process involves using materials like rammed earth, cob, or earthbags. Earth-sheltered homes take advantage of thermal mass, meaning the walls and roof absorb heat during the day and release it at night, keeping the interior temperature consistent. This design greatly reduces the need for external heating or cooling, making it ideal for off-grid living.

Challenges include ensuring proper drainage and moisture control to prevent water infiltration and mold growth. Installing an efficient ventilation system is also critical for maintaining air quality in an earth-sheltered home.

Yurts: Simple, Portable, and Traditional

Yurts are circular, tent-like structures that have been used for centuries by nomadic cultures. Modern yurts combine traditional designs with advanced materials, making them a viable option for off-grid homesteads. Yurts are particularly suitable for milder climates, though they can be adapted for cold weather with proper insulation.

The simplicity of yurt construction allows for quick assembly and disassembly, making them ideal for temporary or seasonal use. They are built with a lightweight wooden frame covered by a fabric shell, often reinforced with natural fibers or modern weather-resistant materials.

Yurts can be customized with wood stoves for heating and solar panels for lighting and power. However, they offer less insulation than permanent structures, so additional insulation measures like double-layered walls and insulated flooring may be necessary for cold climates.

Sustainable Building Materials: Wood, Earth, and Natural Fibers

Choosing sustainable building materials is an integral part of constructing an off-grid home. The right materials minimize environmental impact, reduce costs, and provide excellent insulation and durability.

Wood: Renewable and Versatile

Wood is a renewable resource and one of the most versatile building materials available. Local timber can be used for framing, cladding, and finishing, reducing the carbon footprint associated with transportation. Hardwoods are durable and resistant to pests, making them ideal for structural beams and outdoor decks, while softwoods like pine are lightweight and suitable for interior walls and framing.

Properly treating wood with natural sealants like linseed oil or borate treatments can help protect against moisture, insects, and decay. Using reclaimed wood from old buildings or barns is another sustainable option that adds character and reduces the need for new materials.

Earth-Based Materials: Rammed Earth, Cob, and Earthbags

Rammed Earth: This method involves compacting layers of damp soil between forms to create thick, solid walls. Rammed earth construction is highly sustainable, as it uses local soil and minimal additives like lime or cement for stabilization. The walls provide excellent thermal mass, making them ideal for maintaining comfortable temperatures in both hot and cold climates.

Cob: Cob construction uses a mixture of clay, sand, straw, and water, sculpted by hand to form walls. Cob homes are sustainable and have a unique, organic aesthetic. They also offer high thermal mass, although they require time to dry and cure properly. Cob structures are particularly suitable for mild or arid climates where moisture management is easier.

Earthbags: Earthbag homes use bags filled with soil and stacked like bricks. These bags are tamped down to form solid walls, and the structure is then covered with a protective plaster layer. Earthbags are adaptable and can be used to build curved walls or even domed roofs, making them versatile and earthquake-resistant. This method is suitable for homesteads with access to abundant soil and sand.

Natural Fibers and Insulation Materials: Straw Bales and Hempcrete

Straw Bales: Straw bale construction involves stacking tightly bound bales of straw within a wooden frame to create thick, insulated walls. These walls are then plastered with clay or lime for protection. Straw bales are highly insulating, renewable, and cost-effective, making them ideal for cold climates where maintaining warmth is crucial.

Hempcrete: Hempcrete is a mixture of hemp fibers, lime, and water, forming a lightweight, insulating material that is durable and breathable. It is a sustainable alternative to concrete and offers good insulation and fire resistance. Hempcrete works well in both hot and cold climates but requires an additional structural frame, as it is not load-bearing.

Insulation and Weatherproofing for Extreme Climates

Proper insulation and weatherproofing are critical for off-grid homes, especially those located in areas with harsh or unpredictable weather. Effective insulation reduces energy consumption, while weatherproofing protects the structure from moisture and temperature extremes.

Natural Insulation Options: Wool, Straw, and Cellulose

Wool: Sheep's wool is a natural, breathable insulation material that is sustainable and effective at regulating temperature and moisture. Wool insulation can be installed in walls, roofs, and floors, offering excellent performance in both hot and cold climates. It is naturally fire-retardant and resistant to mold, making it a suitable choice for off-grid homes.

Straw: Straw bale walls provide thick, high-insulation properties, ideal for retaining heat in winter and keeping interiors cool in summer. Straw is also affordable and renewable, making it a great option for eco-friendly builds. However, it must be kept dry to prevent rot, so proper cladding and moisture barriers are essential.

Cellulose: Made from recycled paper products, cellulose insulation is another sustainable option. It is treated with fire retardants and pest-resistant compounds, making it safe for home use. Cellulose works well for insulating walls and attics, but it requires a blower for installation, which may necessitate off-grid equipment like a generator or solar power setup.

Modern and Hybrid Insulation Techniques: Spray Foam and SIPs

Spray Foam: While not as eco-friendly as natural options, spray foam provides high R-value insulation and seals gaps effectively, preventing air leaks. It is suitable for extreme climates where maximizing insulation is crucial, particularly in roofs and wall cavities. Off-grid homesteaders using spray foam should be mindful of its environmental impact and choose low-VOC (volatile organic compounds) options when possible.

Structural Insulated Panels (SIPs): SIPs are prefabricated panels made of foam insulation sandwiched between two structural boards. They are easy to assemble and provide a high level of insulation. SIPs are efficient for building energy-tight structures quickly but require careful planning and transportation logistics for off-grid locations.

Weatherproofing for Moisture Control: Barriers and Ventilation Systems

Moisture Barriers: Installing moisture barriers, such as house wraps or bitumen membranes, helps protect walls and foundations from water damage. These barriers prevent moisture from penetrating the building envelope while allowing vapor to escape, reducing the risk of mold and rot.

Proper Roof Design: Roofing is a critical aspect of weatherproofing. In areas with heavy rain or snow, designing a roof with a steep pitch helps shed water and prevent accumulation. Using durable materials like metal roofing provides long-term protection and reflects heat in hot climates. Ensure gutters and drainage systems are properly designed to direct water away from the foundation.

Ventilation Systems for Extreme Climates: Passive and Active Techniques

Passive Ventilation: Passive systems, such as strategically placed windows and vents, allow for natural airflow, helping regulate indoor temperatures and moisture levels without the need for energy. Cross-ventilation, where windows are placed on opposite sides of a structure, allows air to flow freely and reduces the need for mechanical systems.

Thermal Mass and Insulation: In cold climates, combining passive solar design with materials that have high thermal mass (like stone, brick, or rammed earth) can store and release heat efficiently. Orienting the home to maximize sunlight exposure during the winter months while shading windows in summer helps regulate temperature year-round.

Active Ventilation Systems: For extreme heat or humidity, active systems like solar-powered exhaust fans or heat recovery ventilators (HRVs) provide efficient climate control. HRVs can exchange stale indoor air with fresh outdoor air while retaining heat, making them an effective solution for airtight homes in cold climates.

Sealing Gaps and Improving Efficiency: Caulking and Weather Stripping

Gaps around windows, doors, and other openings can lead to significant energy loss. Use caulking to seal cracks around frames and foundations and weather stripping around doors and windows to reduce air leaks. This simple yet effective method improves the overall efficiency of your insulation and helps maintain a stable indoor climate.

Hybrid and Alternative Building Techniques for Extreme Conditions

Off-grid homesteaders may benefit from exploring hybrid and alternative building techniques that combine traditional methods with modern innovations for maximum efficiency and sustainability.

Hybrid Cabins: Mixing Traditional and Modern Methods

Hybrid cabins combine traditional timber framing with modern materials like SIPs, straw bales, or insulated concrete forms (ICFs). These combinations offer the rustic appeal of cabins with enhanced energy efficiency and quicker construction times. Hybrid cabins are ideal for those who want a balance of aesthetics and performance.

Incorporating solar passive design—positioning the home to capture the sun's heat in winter while shading it in summer—can greatly reduce energy needs for heating and cooling. Additional elements like thermal mass floors (using stone or concrete) help store and radiate heat.

Using Local and Recycled Materials for Unique Homes: Earth and Salvaged Wood

Building with local materials like stone, wood, or clay not only reduces costs but also minimizes environmental impact. Stones gathered from the site can be used for foundations, retaining walls, or flooring, while clay can be turned into cob for walls.

Recycled materials such as reclaimed wood, metal, or even repurposed windows and doors add character and sustainability to the build. Using salvaged materials requires careful planning and craftsmanship but can create a unique, resource-efficient structure.

Alternative Housing Designs: Geodesic Domes and Straw Bale Homes

Geodesic Domes: These structures are highly efficient due to their spherical shape, which reduces surface area and conserves energy. Geodesic domes can be built using lightweight materials like metal pipes and covered with insulating materials like foam panels. They are structurally strong, making them ideal for areas prone to high winds or earthquakes.

Straw Bale Homes: Straw bale construction is becoming increasingly popular due to its affordability and insulating properties. Straw bale walls are thick and provide excellent thermal insulation, making them suitable for both hot and cold climates. They can be finished with clay or lime plaster, offering a natural and breathable wall system.

Balancing Aesthetics and Functionality in Off-Grid Homes

The choice of housing type and materials greatly influences not only the functionality but also the aesthetic appeal of your off-grid home. Balancing these factors helps create a comfortable and efficient space that also feels personalized.

Integrating Natural Landscapes into Design:

Working with the existing landscape, such as building into a hillside or using natural materials found on the site, creates a harmonious and sustainable living environment. Incorporate natural elements like stone pathways, wooden beams, or planted roofs to blend the structure with its surroundings.

Living Roofs: Adding a green roof covered with grass or native plants helps improve insulation, manage rainwater runoff, and integrate the home aesthetically with the landscape. Living roofs are particularly beneficial for earth-sheltered homes and cabins.

Creating Comfortable, Efficient Interiors:

Maximize space in small or unusual structures like yurts or tiny homes with multifunctional furniture and built-in storage. Efficient layouts that use every inch of space reduce the need for large homes and help manage heating and cooling more effectively.

Incorporate natural light through strategically placed windows and skylights to create bright, comfortable interiors without relying on artificial lighting during the day.

Conclusion: Building Sustainable and Efficient Off-Grid Housing

Choosing the right type of off-grid housing and building materials is essential for creating a sustainable and efficient homestead. By exploring options such as cabins, tiny homes, earth-sheltered structures, and yurts, and selecting sustainable materials like wood, earth, and natural fibers, you can design a home that meets your needs and integrates harmoniously with the environment. Insulating and weatherproofing your structure properly ensures that it will withstand extreme climates and provide comfort year-round.

In the next chapter, we will explore off-grid heating and cooling systems, focusing on how to design and implement energy-efficient solutions using solar, wood stoves, and passive techniques.

Chapter 14: Constructing Safe Wilderness Housing

When building a shelter in a wilderness setting, safety, durability, and efficiency are the top priorities. Whether you're constructing a temporary refuge or a long-term homestead, knowing the right techniques ensures that your shelter can withstand harsh weather conditions, wildlife encounters, and other environmental challenges. This chapter provides a step-by-step guide to building a basic wilderness shelter, methods for securing it against wildlife and weather, and strategies for improving your shelter with insulation, solar panels, and water systems.

Step-by-Step Guide to Building a Basic Shelter

Constructing a basic wilderness shelter involves careful planning and the use of locally available materials. The goal is to create a structure that is sturdy, protective, and adaptable to the environment.

Choosing a Suitable Location:

Elevation: Build on slightly elevated ground to avoid flooding and ensure good drainage. Avoid valleys and depressions where water can accumulate during rain.

Wind Protection: Choose a spot that offers natural windbreaks, such as behind a cluster of trees, large rocks, or hillsides. This will reduce the impact of strong winds and help retain heat inside the shelter.

Sunlight and Shade: In cold climates, orient the shelter to capture the most sunlight during the day. In hot climates, prioritize building in shaded areas to keep the interior cool.

Gathering and Preparing Materials:

Collect logs, branches, and large stones as the main structural elements. Use fallen trees or dead wood when possible to minimize environmental impact.

For waterproofing and insulation, gather leaves, pine needles, grass, and bark. These materials provide a natural barrier against the elements when layered properly.

If available, use tarp or plastic sheeting for an extra waterproof layer, especially for the roof.

Building the Frame:

Construct an A-frame or lean-to structure, depending on the available materials and weather conditions:

A-Frame: This design is simple and effective for both warmth and stability. Use two long logs to form a triangular frame, securing the top ends together with rope or vines. Place smaller branches horizontally across the frame to form the roof.

Lean-To: A lean-to is quicker to build and works well for temporary shelters. Find a sturdy tree or pole to support the structure, then lean branches against it to form an angled roof.

Adding Insulation and Waterproofing:

Cover the frame with layers of leaves, branches, and grasses. For best results, apply multiple layers, starting with larger branches to create a base, then adding finer materials like leaves or pine needles for insulation.

Use natural materials like moss to fill gaps and create an airtight seal. If using a tarp or plastic sheet, secure it over the roof and weigh down the edges with stones or logs to keep it in place during high winds.

Techniques for Securing Housing Against Wildlife and Weather

Ensuring that your wilderness shelter is secure involves building it to withstand harsh weather conditions and protecting it from potential wildlife encounters. Below are techniques for reinforcing your shelter's defenses.

Strengthening the Shelter Against Wind and Rain:

Build the shelter with a low profile to minimize wind resistance. A-frame structures are naturally wind-resistant, but if you opt for a lean-to, make sure the slanted side faces the prevailing wind direction.

Use stakes or ropes to anchor the shelter securely to the ground. Drive stakes into the ground at the base of the shelter's walls, or tie the frame to nearby trees using sturdy cord or vines.

Create an overhang with the roof to direct rain away from the entrance and walls. Adding a small trench around the shelter can help channel rainwater and prevent flooding.

Protecting the Shelter from Wildlife:

Food Storage: Wildlife is often attracted to food, so keep any food supplies stored away from the shelter. Use bear-proof containers if available, or hang food in a tree at least 10-15 feet off the ground and several feet away from the trunk.

Perimeter Barriers: Establish a perimeter around the shelter using natural deterrents like thorny bushes or piles of branches. These barriers can discourage animals from approaching too closely.

Scent Marking: Animals like bears, wolves, and smaller scavengers are sensitive to scents. Burn a small fire at a safe distance from the shelter to create a smoke barrier, which helps keep animals away. Avoid cooking inside the shelter to minimize attracting wildlife.

Enhancing Structural Integrity for Storms:

Reinforce the walls of the shelter with additional layers of branches and logs, increasing the thickness to help resist wind and rain. Using rocks at the base of the walls adds stability and weight, reducing the risk of collapse during strong winds.

In cold or snowy regions, build snow walls around the shelter's perimeter to block wind and insulate the structure further. If snow is not available, use stacked logs or earth mounds to achieve a similar effect.

Improving Your Shelter with Insulation, Solar Panels, and Water Systems

Once the basic shelter is established and secured, adding improvements such as insulation, solar panels, and water systems can enhance its comfort and sustainability, especially for long-term use.

Upgrading Insulation for Extreme Climates:

For cold climates, line the interior walls with wool blankets, animal hides, or additional natural materials like straw or dried leaves. These materials provide excellent insulation, helping to retain heat.

Install a double-layer wall system by adding an outer frame to the existing walls and filling the gap with insulating materials. This technique traps heat within the structure and provides an added buffer against the cold.

In hot climates, focus on ventilation. Install ventilation holes near the roofline to allow hot air to escape, and use reflective materials like aluminum foil or light-colored tarps to deflect sunlight.

Installing Solar Panels for Off-Grid Energy:

Solar panels are a practical solution for generating electricity in remote areas. For wilderness shelters, choose portable solar panel kits that can be easily set up and taken down. These kits typically include lightweight panels, a battery, and an inverter for powering small appliances or lighting.

Mount the panels on a frame angled to capture maximum sunlight exposure throughout the day. Ensure the mounting system is secure and stable, using stakes or heavy objects to anchor it against wind.

Connect the solar panels to a battery bank that stores energy for use at night or during cloudy periods. Using LED lights and low-power devices maximizes efficiency and extends battery life.

Establishing a Water Collection System:

Rainwater Harvesting: Collecting rainwater is an effective way to ensure a steady water supply in wilderness areas. Set up a rainwater catchment system using the shelter's roof by attaching gutters or angled tarps that direct water into storage barrels or collapsible tanks.

Install a basic filtration system at the collection point to remove large debris. For drinking water, further purify it using portable filters, boiling, or chemical treatments as discussed in Chapter 11.

In areas with low rainfall, dig a shallow well or a natural seepage pit near water sources like creeks. Line the pit with stones and install a hand pump if possible to create a simple and accessible water source.

Creating a Sustainable Heat Source: Wood Stoves and Passive Solar Heating:

Wood Stoves: If the shelter is built for long-term use, installing a small wood stove provides reliable heating and cooking capabilities. Make sure the stove has a chimney and flue to vent smoke safely outside. Surround the stove with a heat-resistant barrier, such as stone or metal, to protect the walls.

Passive Solar Heating: Design the shelter with south-facing windows (in the northern hemisphere) or north-facing windows (in the southern hemisphere) to capture the sun's heat during the day. Using materials like stone floors or walls helps absorb and release heat gradually, maintaining warmth throughout the night.

Insulate the area around windows with removable covers made from canvas or wool, which can be rolled down during the night or cold days to retain heat and pulled up during warm, sunny days for light and warmth.

Weatherproofing and Climate Adaptations for Long-Term Wilderness Shelters

Adapting your shelter to withstand long-term exposure to wilderness conditions ensures its durability and livability. Techniques for effective weatherproofing and climate-specific adaptations are crucial for maintaining a comfortable and safe environment.

Weatherproofing for Rainy and Snowy Conditions:

Roof Reinforcement: In areas prone to heavy snow or rain, strengthen the roof with additional rafters and crossbeams to support extra weight. Waterproof the roof using a combination of tarps and natural materials like bark or reeds.

Snow Guards and Awnings: For snowy regions, install snow guards on the roof to prevent large accumulations from sliding off suddenly. Build awnings over doorways and windows to keep them clear and accessible during storms.

Apply a waterproof sealant to wood surfaces to prevent rot and degradation. Regularly inspect and reapply as needed, especially before the onset of the rainy or snowy season.

Preparing for Seasonal Temperature Changes:

In climates with hot summers and cold winters, build removable wall panels that can be adjusted based on the season. Use lightweight, insulating materials like straw for summer panels that can be removed to increase ventilation, and heavier materials like wool or canvas for winter.

Create a cool storage area within or adjacent to the shelter by digging into the ground. The earth naturally maintains cooler temperatures, making this space suitable for storing perishable items and providing a cool retreat during hot weather.

Insulate the shelter's floor using rugs, straw mats, or wooden platforms to create a barrier between the living area and the cold ground. This also helps keep the shelter dry and free from dampness, improving overall comfort.

Improving Wildlife Security Measures:

Install metal grates or screens over windows and entry points to keep smaller animals and insects from entering. This is especially important in areas with bears or other large animals that may be attracted to the smell of food.

Keep the shelter area clear of debris and stack firewood at a safe distance to avoid creating habitats for pests near your living space. This practice also reduces fire hazards.

For long-term shelters, building an external fence around the perimeter can further deter wildlife and create a buffer zone for safety.

Adding Functional Extensions: Storage, Kitchens, and Outdoor Living Spaces

Expanding your shelter to include functional spaces like storage areas, outdoor kitchens, and workspaces enhances the usability and comfort of your wilderness home.

Constructing a Storage Area:

Building an outdoor shed adjacent to the shelter provides storage for tools, firewood, and food supplies. Use materials like wood and stone to create a structure that blends with the environment while remaining secure against weather and animals.

Elevated storage platforms can be used to keep supplies dry and safe from rodents. Elevating these platforms and covering them with a tarp or wooden roof ensures that they remain accessible during heavy rains or snow.

Creating an Outdoor Kitchen Space:

An outdoor kitchen reduces smoke and fire risks inside the shelter. Set up a fire pit or rocket stove surrounded by stones for cooking, and build a wood shelter nearby to keep fuel dry.

Install a simple canopy or tarp structure over the kitchen area to provide shade during hot weather and protection from rain. Organize cooking tools and supplies on a hanging rack or within a storage bench to keep them accessible and safe from wildlife.

Establishing Comfortable Outdoor Living Areas:

Adding a covered porch or deck area enhances the functionality of the shelter by providing outdoor space for relaxation, work, or socializing. Construct the deck with wood planks, and secure it with stakes or rocks to withstand wind and storms.

Integrate natural seating using logs or stones, and create pathways with local stones or wood chips to maintain clean and dry access around the shelter.

Building Advanced Systems for Long-Term Off-Grid Living

To fully sustain an off-grid wilderness home, consider building advanced systems like solar energy setups, water filtration systems, and integrated heating solutions.

Integrating a Solar Power System:

Expand the solar setup by adding additional panels and batteries as needed. Mount panels on adjustable stands that allow for seasonal tilting to optimize sun exposure throughout the year.

Use the stored solar energy to power LED lighting, small appliances, and communication devices. Set up a battery bank protected from the elements in a secure and insulated housing area.

Include a backup power source, such as a wind turbine or a small generator, to ensure continuous power supply during cloudy periods or winter months when sunlight may be limited.

Installing an Advanced Water Filtration and Collection System:

Upgrade rainwater harvesting by adding a first flush diverter to filter out initial contaminants before water enters the storage tanks. Install a multi-stage filtration system with activated carbon and UV light to purify water for drinking.

Expand storage capacity by connecting multiple tanks and placing them on elevated platforms for gravity-fed water systems that provide consistent pressure without the need for electric pumps.

Enhancing Heating and Cooling Efficiency:

Integrate a thermal mass heating system by building a stone wall or earthen bench next to the wood stove. This design captures and slowly releases heat, providing warmth long after the fire has died down.

Add insulated window shutters that can be closed during winter nights to retain heat and opened during the day to allow in sunlight. For summer cooling, build awnings or shade screens to reduce indoor temperatures and improve comfort.

Consider building an underground cooling tube system that draws cooler air from underground into the shelter. This passive cooling technique is effective in hot climates and does not rely on external energy sources.

Conclusion: Constructing a Durable and Functional Wilderness Shelter

Building a safe and functional wilderness shelter involves understanding your environment and making smart choices about materials, construction techniques, and security measures. Whether you are building a temporary refuge or a long-term homestead, these steps help ensure that your shelter is durable, efficient, and secure against wildlife and weather. Improving the shelter with modern systems like solar panels, advanced insulation, and water filtration transforms it into a sustainable living space suitable for off-grid living.

In the next chapter, we'll explore off-grid energy solutions, focusing on the best methods for generating and storing power using renewable energy sources like solar, wind, and micro-hydro systems.

Chapter 15: Off-Grid Kitchen and Cooking Techniques

Cooking off-grid requires adapting to methods that do not rely on conventional electricity, while also ensuring that your kitchen setup can handle food preservation and long-term storage. In this chapter, we'll explore various cooking methods such as solar ovens, wood stoves, and campfire setups, all of which are designed for energy efficiency and sustainability. We will also cover techniques for preserving food, including canning, drying, fermenting, and smoking, as well as strategies for setting up a pantry for long-term food storage to maintain a well-stocked off-grid kitchen.

Cooking Without Electricity: Solar Ovens, Wood Stoves, and Campfire Setups

Cooking off-grid means finding alternative ways to prepare meals that are efficient, sustainable, and environmentally friendly. Below are some of the most effective methods for off-grid cooking.

Solar Ovens: Harnessing the Sun's Energy

How Solar Ovens Work: Solar ovens use reflective surfaces to concentrate sunlight into a cooking chamber, trapping heat to cook food. These ovens are especially useful in sunny climates and can reach temperatures of 250-350°F (120-180°C), sufficient for baking, roasting, and slow cooking.

Building a DIY Solar Oven: For a simple solar oven, line the interior of a box with aluminum foil to reflect sunlight, and place a glass or clear plastic lid on top to create a greenhouse effect. Angle the box toward the sun using a reflective surface (e.g., a piece of aluminum sheet) to focus more light into the chamber.

Advantages and Limitations: Solar ovens are excellent for fuel-free cooking, but they depend entirely on sunlight, making them less reliable during cloudy or rainy periods. They are ideal for baking bread, cooking stews, or dehydrating fruits and vegetables.

Wood Stoves: A Classic Off-Grid Cooking Method

Types of Wood Stoves: Wood stoves are versatile and provide both heating and cooking capabilities. Rocket stoves and traditional cast-iron wood stoves are popular off-grid options. Rocket stoves are efficient, using minimal wood while maximizing heat output, and are perfect for quick cooking. Traditional wood stoves, on the other hand, offer more cooking space and can double as a heat source for your shelter.

Cooking Techniques with Wood Stoves: Use cast iron cookware, such as Dutch ovens and skillets, which retain heat well and are durable. You can bake, fry, or simmer food using the stove's various temperature zones—placing pots closer to the fire for higher heat and further away for simmering.

Managing Fuel Efficiency: Collect and store dry wood, ideally hardwoods like oak, maple, or hickory, which burn longer and hotter. Keep kindling and small twigs on hand for starting fires quickly. Learning to control the airflow and damper on the stove is crucial for managing cooking temperatures and fuel efficiency.

Campfire Setups: Cooking Over an Open Flame

Building a Safe and Effective Campfire: Choose a flat, open area away from flammable materials. Dig a fire pit and surround it with rocks to contain the fire and reflect heat. A tripod grill or a spit can be used for cooking meats, while flat stones can be heated for cooking flatbreads or eggs.

Cooking Tools for Campfires: Use a cast-iron skillet, Dutch oven, or grill grate for versatility. Hanging a pot from a tripod over the flames allows for controlled boiling and simmering. Keep a long-handled spatula or tongs for turning food safely, and always have a bucket of water or sand nearby for fire safety.

Campfire Cooking Tips: Cooking over a campfire requires attention and control over the flame size. Use hot coals rather than direct flames for consistent heat when grilling or baking. Cover pots with lids to retain heat and minimize cooking time.

Food Preservation Methods: Canning, Drying, Fermenting, and Smoking

Preserving food off-grid is crucial for long-term sustainability and minimizing food waste. Each preservation method has its own benefits and is suitable for different types of food.

Canning: Storing Food for the Long Term

Water Bath Canning: This method is ideal for high-acid foods like fruits, jams, and pickles. Boil jars filled with food in a water bath to create a vacuum seal, which prevents bacterial growth. Ensure jars and lids are sterilized properly before use to avoid contamination.

Pressure Canning: For low-acid foods like vegetables, meats, and soups, pressure canning is necessary to reach the temperatures needed to kill harmful bacteria like botulism. Use a pressure canner, which allows you to cook jars at high pressure, ensuring a safe seal. Follow recipes closely to ensure that proper temperatures and times are maintained for safe storage.

Storing Canned Goods: Store sealed jars in a cool, dark place, such as a root cellar or pantry, to prolong shelf life. Check seals periodically and rotate jars to use older preserves first. Properly canned foods can last 1-3 years, providing a reliable food supply during winter or dry periods.

Drying and Dehydrating: A Low-Energy Preservation Method

Air Drying and Sun Drying: For foods like herbs, peppers, and certain fruits, air drying is a simple and effective method. Hang herbs or string up slices of fruit in a well-ventilated area that receives plenty of sunlight. Protect the food from insects by covering it with mesh or netting.

Dehydrators and Solar Drying: Using a solar dehydrator, which can be built with wooden frames and mesh screens, speeds up the drying process by concentrating sunlight. Electric or solar-powered dehydrators are also available, providing consistent drying temperatures for making jerky, dried fruits, and vegetables.

Storing Dried Foods: Store dried foods in airtight containers or vacuum-sealed bags to keep out moisture and pests. Properly dried foods can last up to 6-12 months and are lightweight and easy to transport, making them ideal for off-grid living and emergency rations.

Fermenting: A Nutrient-Preserving Technique

Fermenting Vegetables: Fermentation not only preserves food but also enhances its nutritional value by introducing beneficial bacteria. Common fermented foods include sauerkraut, kimchi, pickles, and fermented carrots. Use a brine solution (water and salt) and keep vegetables submerged in an anaerobic (oxygen-free) environment using fermentation weights.

Yogurt and Dairy Fermentation: For off-grid homesteads with dairy animals, fermenting milk into yogurt or cheese is a practical way to extend its shelf life. Use a simple setup, like a thermos or insulated container, to maintain a warm temperature during the fermentation process.

Storing Fermented Foods: Fermented foods should be kept in cool, dark places or refrigerated once the fermentation process is complete. They typically last several months, making them valuable for off-grid kitchens that need nutrient-rich, long-lasting foods.

Smoking: Preserving and Flavoring Meats

Cold Smoking vs. Hot Smoking: Cold smoking preserves food by drying it at low temperatures (below 90°F), while hot smoking cooks and flavors meat at higher temperatures (150-200°F). Cold smoking is ideal for fish, sausages, and jerky, while hot smoking is better for immediate consumption.

Building a Smoker: An off-grid smoker can be made using a barrel, wooden box, or even a pit in the ground. The key is to create a separate fire chamber where the smoke can be channeled through to the food without direct heat contact. Use hardwoods like hickory, oak, or mesquite for a rich, smoky flavor.

Storing Smoked Foods: Properly smoked meats should be dried and stored in cool, dry conditions. Vacuum-sealing or wrapping them tightly in butcher paper further extends their shelf life.

Setting Up a Pantry for Long-Term Food Storage

A well-organized pantry is essential for maintaining a reliable food supply in an off-grid environment. By incorporating the right storage techniques and organizing your food supplies efficiently, you can maximize your resources and ensure that your kitchen is prepared for any situation.

Designing a Pantry Space:

Choose a cool, dark, and dry location for your pantry, such as a root cellar or a well-ventilated storage room. The goal is to maintain a stable temperature, ideally between 50-60°F, to prevent spoilage. Insulate the space if necessary to protect it from extreme temperatures.

Install shelves and storage bins to keep foods organized and easily accessible. Use sturdy, adjustable shelving that can handle the weight of heavy jars and containers. Label each section clearly for easy access.

Storing Dry Goods: Grains, Beans, and Flours:

Grains and Legumes: Grains like rice, oats, and wheat, as well as beans, are off-grid staples due to their long shelf life. Store them in airtight containers or food-grade buckets with oxygen absorbers to extend freshness. Consider rotating them periodically to maintain their quality.

Flours and Powders: Flours, baking powders, and other dry ingredients should be stored in sealed containers to keep out moisture and pests. If possible, vacuum-seal flours to reduce the risk of spoilage and extend shelf life.

Storing Preserved Foods: Jars, Cans, and Dried Goods

Organizing Canned Goods: Arrange canned foods by type and date, keeping the oldest jars at the front to ensure proper rotation. Check seals regularly and remove any jars showing signs of spoilage, such as bulging lids or rust.

Dried Foods: Place dried fruits, vegetables, and herbs in glass jars or vacuum-sealed bags to prevent exposure to air and pests. Keep these in a dark section of the pantry to avoid sunlight, which can degrade nutrients.

Storing Oils, Fats, and Dairy Products:

Oils and Fats: Store cooking oils in opaque glass bottles to prevent oxidation from light exposure. Animal fats, like lard or tallow, should be stored in cool conditions and can be preserved for extended periods by rendering and storing in airtight jars.

Dairy Products: Cheese and butter can be stored long-term through methods like waxing (for cheese) or creating ghee (clarified butter). Ghee is shelf-stable and can last for months if kept in a sealed container at a cool temperature.

Preventing Pests and Maintaining Pantry Hygiene:

Pest Control: Keep pests out by using natural repellents like bay leaves or peppermint oil near shelves. Store dry goods in metal or thick plastic containers that are rodent-proof. Inspect food supplies regularly for signs of contamination or pests.

Cleaning and Maintenance: Clean the pantry area regularly to prevent the buildup of crumbs or spills that attract insects and rodents. Sweep floors, wipe down shelves, and ensure containers remain sealed. Rotate foods periodically to minimize the risk of spoilage.

Expanding Your Pantry: Growing and Preserving for Self-Sufficiency

A comprehensive off-grid pantry includes not only stored food but also a plan for continuously replenishing supplies through gardening, foraging, and livestock management.

Growing Your Own Pantry Staples:

Root Vegetables: Potatoes, carrots, onions, and beets are long-lasting crops that store well in a root cellar. Harvest them in late summer or fall, and store them in crates filled with sawdust or sand to maintain freshness.

Herbs and Spices: Dried herbs are essential for flavor and medicinal purposes. Grow and dry your own oregano, basil, thyme, and other herbs, and store them in airtight containers. Consider growing garlic and ginger for both cooking and health benefits.

Integrating Livestock Products into Your Food Storage:

Egg Preservation: Fresh eggs can be stored without refrigeration using methods like water glassing (submerging eggs in a lime solution) or freezing them after beating. These methods extend the usability of eggs for baking and cooking.

Curing Meats: Utilize livestock to create preserved meats like jerky, salami, or bacon. These cured products can be smoked, air-dried, or packed in salt for long-term storage.

Establishing a Seasonal Storage Cycle:

Plan your pantry stocking around seasonal harvests, preserving fruits, vegetables, and meats when they are abundant. Keep a calendar to track canning, drying, and fermenting schedules to optimize your time and resources.

Rotate preserved foods into your daily diet, replenishing the pantry with new batches as old ones are used. This cycle ensures that you always have fresh supplies and helps you avoid waste.

Managing a Sustainable Off-Grid Kitchen

Sustaining an off-grid kitchen requires strategic management and adaptability to changing conditions.

Water Supply Management:

Ensure that your water collection and filtration systems are efficient enough to provide a steady supply for cooking, cleaning, and food preservation. Setting up an on-demand water heater powered by solar or wood can provide hot water for washing dishes and processing foods like canned vegetables.

Planning for Emergencies and Shortages:

Maintain an emergency food kit with portable, non-perishable items like dried beans, rice, jerky, and canned goods for situations when fresh supplies are limited. Rotate emergency rations regularly to keep them fresh and usable.

Store additional cooking fuel sources, such as propane or charcoal, for periods when gathering firewood may not be possible due to weather or availability.

Setting Up a Food Exchange System:

Building a network with neighboring homesteaders or local markets allows you to trade surplus produce or preserved foods. An exchange system not only diversifies your food supply but also provides an opportunity to barter for other essential items.

Consider organizing seasonal community canning events where multiple families come together to share resources and techniques, increasing efficiency and building community ties.

Long-Term Strategies for an Efficient Off-Grid Kitchen

As your off-grid homestead becomes established, refining and improving your kitchen systems ensures efficiency and sustainability.

Installing a Root Cellar for Fresh Food Storage:

Root cellars are ideal for storing vegetables, fruits, and fermented foods. Build a partially underground storage space with proper ventilation to maintain stable temperatures and humidity levels. Insulate the cellar using straw bales, clay, or stone to keep it functional year-round.

Organize the root cellar with shelving and hanging racks for different types of produce and preserve. Label each section clearly and keep a log of stored items to monitor freshness and usage.

Expanding Solar and Wood Cooking Systems:

Upgrade solar ovens with larger panels or reflective surfaces to cook bigger meals or multiple dishes simultaneously. Incorporate a thermal battery (a heat-retaining material like stone) in your solar setup to continue cooking or baking even after the sun sets.

Enhance your wood stove by adding water heating coils or an attached oven box for baking bread or roasting meat, making it a multi-purpose tool that supports both cooking and heating needs.

Incorporating Alternative Preservation Methods:

Explore alternative methods like root vegetable clamping (burying vegetables in the ground with insulating materials like straw) or building a solar dehydrator for large-scale drying of fruits, vegetables, and herbs.

Expand fermentation processes by making fermented drinks like kombucha, kefir, or cider, adding variety to your pantry while utilizing seasonal produce.

Conclusion: Mastering the Off-Grid Kitchen

An efficient off-grid kitchen integrates various cooking techniques, food preservation methods, and storage strategies to ensure sustainability and adaptability. By setting up systems like solar ovens, wood stoves, and well-organized pantries, you create a resilient and resourceful kitchen that can handle the demands of off-grid living. Through a combination of traditional skills and modern adaptations, your kitchen becomes the heart of your homestead, providing sustenance and stability.

In the next chapter, we'll explore water management systems, focusing on the best practices for collecting, purifying, and distributing water efficiently across your homestead.

Chapter 16: DIY Off-Grid Plumbing Systems

Off-grid living requires innovative solutions for water management, especially when traditional municipal systems are unavailable. Setting up an effective off-grid plumbing system involves distributing water efficiently, managing wastewater, and ensuring systems are sustainable and low maintenance. In this chapter, we will explore how to set up plumbing for water distribution, implement composting toilets and greywater recycling systems, and provide essential tips for maintaining and repairing these systems without relying on professional services.

Setting Up Plumbing for Water Distribution Without Municipal Systems

The backbone of any off-grid homestead is a reliable and efficient water distribution system that supplies water for drinking, cooking, washing, and irrigation. Setting up such a system involves using natural water sources and designing a network that maximizes efficiency while minimizing reliance on external power sources.

Water Sources and Initial Setup:

Wells: Drilling a well is a common method for accessing groundwater. Once a well is established, a hand pump or solar-powered pump can be installed to draw water into the homestead's plumbing system. Solar pumps are ideal for off-grid setups, providing a sustainable way to bring water from deep underground to storage tanks or directly into the home.

Rainwater Collection: Incorporate rainwater harvesting by directing runoff from rooftops into storage tanks or cisterns. This water can be filtered and used for various household and irrigation purposes. Install gravity-fed systems where possible, using elevated tanks to create natural pressure for water distribution.

Piping and Plumbing Network Design:

Choose PVC, PEX, or copper pipes for the plumbing network, as these materials are durable and resistant to corrosion. PVC and PEX are easier to work with and ideal for off-grid setups due to their flexibility and affordability.

Design a centralized distribution point, such as a water manifold, that connects the main water source to different areas like the kitchen, bathroom, and garden. The manifold allows you to control water flow to each area, making maintenance easier.

Where possible, use gravity to feed water into the system. This reduces the need for electric pumps and ensures that water flows consistently. Position storage tanks at an elevated location or build towers that elevate tanks, allowing water to flow naturally through the plumbing network.

Heating Water Off-Grid:

Solar Water Heaters: Solar water heaters use the sun's energy to heat water in insulated tanks. Build a solar water heater by placing black pipes or tanks in a sunny area, where they absorb heat and store warm water for use in showers or dishwashing.

Wood-Fired Water Heaters: In colder climates or for homesteads with abundant wood resources, wood-fired water heaters provide an alternative. These systems involve running water through coils heated by wood stoves, creating a simple and efficient way to access hot water.

Tankless Systems: Off-grid tankless water heaters powered by propane or solar energy offer another option. They heat water on demand, conserving energy and ensuring a steady hot water supply without needing large storage tanks.

Composting Toilets and Greywater Systems for Water Recycling

Managing waste and recycling water is essential for off-grid homesteads. Composting toilets and greywater systems provide sustainable solutions that reduce water usage and create valuable resources like compost and irrigation water.

Composting Toilets: Sustainable and Water-Free Waste Management

How Composting Toilets Work: Composting toilets convert human waste into compost through a natural decomposition process. They require no water, making them ideal for off-grid living. The composting process involves separating liquids and solids, managing odor through ventilation, and maintaining the right balance of carbon-rich (brown) and nitrogen-rich (green) materials.

Types of Composting Toilets:

Self-Contained Units: These are compact systems that can be installed directly in the bathroom. Waste is composted within the unit itself, and the resulting compost can be removed periodically. Self-contained systems are easy to install but have limited capacity.

Central Composting Systems: These involve a toilet connected to a larger composting bin outside the main living area. Waste is transported via pipes, and the larger bin allows for longer composting cycles and greater capacity. These systems are suitable for larger homesteads and minimize odor within the home.

Setting Up and Maintaining a Composting Toilet: Install the toilet with proper ventilation to prevent odors. Ensure that the toilet design includes a mechanism for separating liquids and solids, as this improves the composting process and reduces smell. Use materials like sawdust, peat moss, or coconut coir to add carbon and balance moisture levels. Regularly rotate the compost to aerate it and accelerate decomposition.

Greywater Systems: Recycling Household Water for Irrigation

What is Greywater? Greywater is lightly used water from sinks, showers, and laundry (excluding toilet waste). It can be recycled for irrigation, reducing the need for fresh water. By implementing a greywater system, you can direct this water to your garden, fruit trees, or other non-potable uses.

Setting Up a Basic Greywater System:

Divert water from sinks, showers, and laundry to a settling tank that filters out debris. This tank should include a basic filter like mesh screens or sand filters to remove particles before water is released into the irrigation network.

From the settling tank, direct greywater through perforated pipes into garden beds or drip irrigation systems. Avoid using greywater on edible parts of plants (like leafy greens) and focus on fruit trees, shrubs, or ornamental plants.

Maintaining Greywater Systems: Regularly clean filters and inspect pipes for clogs or leaks. Use biodegradable, environmentally friendly soaps and detergents to ensure that greywater remains safe for plants. Greywater should not be stored for long periods, as it can become anaerobic and create unpleasant odors.

Blackwater Management: Off-Grid Septic and Bio-Digester Systems

While composting toilets manage human waste without water, other waste management systems like bio-digesters can handle blackwater (waste from toilets) in combination with organic kitchen scraps. Bio-digesters convert waste into biogas and compost through anaerobic digestion, providing both a waste solution and a source of renewable energy.

For those using a septic system, install a leach field that disperses wastewater safely underground. Regularly inspect and pump the septic tank to prevent backups and contamination of the surrounding environment.

Maintaining and Repairing Plumbing Systems Off the Grid

An effective off-grid plumbing system requires regular maintenance and a basic understanding of repairs to ensure its longevity and functionality. Here are essential tips for keeping your system running smoothly.

Routine Inspections and Maintenance:

Pipe Checks: Regularly inspect pipes for leaks, especially at connections and joints. PEX piping, commonly used in off-grid systems, is flexible and easy to repair with crimp fittings and clamps. Copper pipes, while durable, may require soldering for repairs, so keeping basic soldering tools and supplies is advisable.

Tank Cleaning: Water storage tanks, including rainwater and greywater tanks, should be cleaned at least once a year. Drain the tank, scrub the interior with a mild solution of vinegar and water, and rinse thoroughly before refilling. This prevents algae growth and keeps the water supply clean.

Pump Maintenance: For systems using pumps, whether solar or hand-operated, ensure the pump and its components are regularly inspected for wear. Solar pumps may require battery checks and panel cleaning to maintain efficiency, while hand pumps should be lubricated and inspected for rust or damage.

Repairing Leaks and Replacing Parts:

Fixing Leaks: Leaks are common in plumbing systems, especially around joints and connections. Keep a stock of pipe clamps, sealants, and replacement fittings for quick repairs. For temporary fixes, rubber patches or epoxy putty can seal leaks until a more permanent repair is possible.

Replacing Valves and Fittings: Valves are critical for controlling water flow. Over time, they may corrode or wear out. Replace faulty valves with brass or plastic fittings designed for off-grid plumbing systems. Make sure to have spare valves and fittings compatible with your piping system (e.g., PEX, PVC) on hand for quick replacements.

Winterizing the System: In colder climates, pipes and tanks must be winterized to prevent freezing. Insulate exposed pipes with foam sleeves or wrapping tape. Drain water lines that are not in use during winter months, and use heat tape on critical lines that must remain operational.

Tools and Kits for Off-Grid Plumbing Repairs:

A basic plumbing toolkit for off-grid living should include:

Pipe wrenches and adjustable wrenches for tightening fittings.

PEX crimping tool and copper pipe cutters for managing different types of pipes.

A soldering kit (torch, flux, and solder) for copper pipe repairs.

Sealant tape, PVC glue, and plumbing putty for sealing leaks and joints.

A multimeter for testing solar pump systems and checking battery connections.

Efficient Water Management Techniques for Off-Grid Systems

Beyond basic setup and maintenance, improving efficiency and planning for expansion ensures a resilient water system capable of handling seasonal changes and growth.

Optimizing Water Usage with Low-Flow Fixtures:

Install low-flow faucets, showerheads, and toilets to reduce overall water consumption. These fixtures are designed to maintain pressure while using less water, conserving resources and extending the capacity of storage tanks.

Use foot-pump or hand-pump faucets for outdoor sinks or gardens, as these provide precise control over water flow, reducing waste. They are also energy-free, aligning with off-grid principles.

Expanding Water Systems for Seasonal Variability:

Install additional rainwater tanks to store surplus water during the rainy season, ensuring reserves for drier months. Multiple tanks can be connected through overflow pipes, allowing for an expanded storage system that can be filled gradually.

Solar-Powered Irrigation Systems: Using solar-powered pumps for garden irrigation maximizes efficiency by providing water directly where it's needed, even in remote areas. Drip irrigation systems connected to greywater or rainwater tanks reduce water loss and support crop growth sustainably.

Planning for Future Upgrades and Expansions:

Design your plumbing system with modularity in mind, allowing for future expansions. Use quick-connect fittings and shut-off valves that make it easier to add new sections, such as additional bathrooms or water points for livestock.

Consider integrating alternative water sources, such as a micro-hydro system or a pond, into your existing setup. These sources provide redundancy, ensuring that if one system fails (e.g., the well runs dry), others can still supply water.

Water Purification and Quality Control in Off-Grid Systems

Ensuring water quality is paramount in off-grid setups. Implementing multiple layers of filtration and testing systems protects against contaminants and ensures that water remains safe for all uses.

Filtration Systems for Off-Grid Water:

For drinking water, set up a multi-stage filtration system that includes sediment filters, activated carbon filters, and UV sterilization units. These systems remove particles, chlorine, heavy metals, and pathogens, providing safe water without reliance on chemicals.

Gravity-fed filters are effective for smaller volumes of water and require no energy source. Ceramic and bio-sand filters are suitable for off-grid homes, as they use natural filtration methods that can be maintained and cleaned regularly.

Testing Water Quality Regularly:

Use portable water testing kits to check for common contaminants such as bacteria, pH levels, and mineral content. Regular testing, especially after heavy rains or seasonal changes, ensures that the water system remains safe and functional.

If water tests reveal contamination, address the issue promptly. For bacterial contamination, boiling or treating water with chlorine tablets or UV purifiers is effective. For chemical contamination, replacing filters or using activated carbon systems can help purify the water.

Emergency Measures for Water Shortages and System Failures:

In case of water shortages, maintain a reserve of potable water in sealed containers that can be accessed quickly. Rotate these reserves periodically to keep them fresh.

Develop an emergency repair plan for critical components like pumps, valves, or tanks. This plan should include instructions for bypassing faulty sections and switching to backup systems (e.g., manual pumps in case of solar pump failure).

Keep additional parts and tools on hand to perform urgent repairs, such as extra pipes, connectors, and sealants. Having a well-organized storage area for these supplies ensures that you can respond quickly to issues.

Integrating Plumbing Systems with Other Off-Grid Infrastructure

A fully integrated off-grid system connects water management with other essential functions, like energy and waste management, to create a cohesive and efficient setup.

Connecting Water Systems to Energy Sources:

Integrate solar panels with your water heating system to power pumps and maintain hot water availability. Use solar-powered well pumps or irrigation systems to reduce dependence on other fuel sources, ensuring a consistent water supply.

If using micro-hydro systems, channel energy from the water flow to power other components of the homestead, such as lighting or small appliances.

Linking Greywater Systems with Gardening and Irrigation:

Design gardens and greenhouses to be directly connected to greywater output, using this recycled water to nourish fruit trees, shrubs, or non-edible plants. This integration reduces water waste and supports sustainable agriculture.

Install composting bins near greywater outlets to compost kitchen waste and provide organic material for soil improvement, further linking systems and maximizing resource efficiency.

Connecting Waste Management Systems with Water Recycling:

Composting toilets and greywater systems should be positioned strategically near the garden or greenhouse areas, making it easier to transport composted material and use recycled water for irrigation.

Use bio-digesters not only for waste management but also for producing biogas, which can be connected to cooking appliances or heaters, creating a loop where water, waste, and energy systems work together.

Conclusion: Designing a Reliable Off-Grid Plumbing System

Establishing an effective and sustainable off-grid plumbing system involves careful planning, consistent maintenance, and the use of appropriate technologies like solar water heaters, greywater recycling, and composting toilets. By integrating these components and ensuring a flexible design, you create a resilient and adaptable water management system capable of supporting long-term off-grid living. Proper maintenance and preparedness for repairs will keep your plumbing system efficient, ensuring that water remains a consistent resource for your homestead.

In the next chapter, we will focus on off-grid heating solutions, exploring how to use wood stoves, solar heating, and other energy-efficient methods to maintain comfortable indoor temperatures year-round.

Chapter 17: Alternative Heating and Cooling Methods

For off-grid living, maintaining comfortable indoor temperatures without relying on traditional energy sources is essential. Heating and cooling methods must be efficient, sustainable, and adaptable to various climates. In this chapter, we explore different heating options like wood stoves, propane systems, and passive solar heating. We'll also look into effective cooling strategies using shade, ventilation, and earth-cooling techniques, providing practical tips on how to maintain indoor climate control efficiently and sustainably.

Heating Options: Wood Stoves, Propane, and Passive Solar Heating

Heating your off-grid home requires finding a balance between energy efficiency, sustainability, and cost. Below are the primary methods for off-grid heating, each suited to different climates and resource availability.

Wood Stoves: A Reliable and Classic Heating Method

Types of Wood Stoves: Wood stoves are one of the most dependable and efficient heating options for off-grid homesteads. Modern wood stoves come in a variety of designs, from traditional cast-iron models to more efficient rocket stoves that use less wood and maximize heat output. Rocket stoves are especially effective in smaller spaces and can be used both for heating and cooking.

Installation and Setup: Place the wood stove centrally within the home to maximize heat distribution. Ensure the stove has an insulated chimney that extends above the roofline to maintain proper ventilation and prevent smoke buildup. Use a fireproof base, such as stone or brick, to protect the flooring and create thermal mass that absorbs and radiates heat.

Fuel Management: Store hardwoods like oak, maple, or hickory, which burn longer and produce more heat than softwoods. Maintain a woodpile sheltered from the elements to keep it dry and ready for use. Efficient stacking and rotation of firewood help manage your fuel supply throughout the season.

Propane Heaters: Efficient and Portable Solutions

Propane Heating Systems: Propane heaters are a practical off-grid heating option, especially in colder climates where maintaining wood supplies might be challenging. They are efficient, produce significant heat output, and can be easily regulated with thermostats. Wall-mounted propane heaters and portable models are available, providing flexibility in placement and usage.

Installation Considerations: Propane heaters must be installed with proper ventilation to ensure safety and reduce carbon monoxide risk. Install carbon monoxide detectors and regularly inspect propane lines for leaks or damage.

Fuel Storage and Usage: Propane tanks should be stored safely outside the home, and backup supplies should be on hand to ensure continuous operation during extreme cold spells. Monitor fuel levels regularly to prevent unexpected shortages.

Passive Solar Heating: Harnessing Natural Sunlight

Principles of Passive Solar Design: Passive solar heating takes advantage of the sun's energy to warm your home without using any fuel. By strategically orienting windows and using building materials that absorb and store heat, passive solar systems can maintain comfortable temperatures throughout the day. South-facing windows (in the northern hemisphere) or north-facing windows (in the southern hemisphere) are critical for maximizing sunlight exposure during winter.

Thermal Mass: Use materials like stone floors, concrete walls, or ceramic tiles to create thermal mass that absorbs sunlight during the day and releases heat at night. These materials stabilize indoor temperatures and reduce the need for additional heating sources.

Designing a Passive Solar System: Install insulated window covers or thermal curtains that can be drawn at night to retain heat. Consider building sunrooms or greenhouses adjacent to living areas, which act as thermal buffers and provide additional space for growing plants.

Combining Heating Systems for Maximum Efficiency:

Combining multiple heating methods ensures you have reliable options depending on weather conditions and fuel availability. For instance, using a wood stove as the primary source and a propane heater as a backup allows for flexibility during particularly cold spells or when wood supplies are low.

Solar thermal collectors, which use the sun to heat water circulated through a system of pipes, can supplement wood stoves or propane systems. This integration reduces reliance on wood and propane, making the system more sustainable.

Cooling Systems Using Shade, Ventilation, and Earth-Cooling Techniques

Cooling off-grid homes efficiently requires strategic use of natural resources like shade, wind, and the earth's stable underground temperatures. The following methods help keep homes comfortable during hot weather without the need for air conditioning.

Shade and Insulation: The First Line of Defense Against Heat

Exterior Shade Structures: Install awnings, pergolas, or shade sails over windows and outdoor living spaces to block direct sunlight. Deciduous trees planted strategically around the home provide seasonal shade; their leaves shield windows in summer but allow sunlight through when they shed in winter.

Reflective Roofing Materials: Use light-colored or reflective roofing materials to deflect sunlight and reduce heat absorption. Applying a white reflective coating to existing roofs can significantly lower indoor temperatures.

Insulation: Properly insulate walls, ceilings, and floors to prevent heat from entering the home. Insulation materials like wool, cellulose, or straw bales are sustainable and effective at maintaining cool interiors during summer.

Ventilation: Natural Airflow for Efficient Cooling

Cross Ventilation: Design the home with windows on opposite sides to allow air to flow freely, creating a cooling breeze. Place louvered windows or ventilation panels at higher points to release hot air that rises naturally.

Wind Catchers and Ventilation Towers: Inspired by traditional Middle Eastern architecture, wind catchers or ventilation towers direct cooler outside air into the home while expelling warm air.

These structures use wind pressure and temperature differences to create a natural flow, reducing the need for mechanical cooling.

Ceiling and Attic Fans: Install solar-powered ceiling fans or attic fans to circulate air efficiently. Attic fans, in particular, help remove hot air trapped in the upper levels of the home, lowering the overall temperature.

Earth-Cooling Techniques: Using the Ground's Stable Temperatures

Earth Tubes: Earth tubes are a simple and effective method for passive cooling. These underground pipes draw cool air from below the surface, where temperatures remain relatively constant. The air is then directed into the home, reducing indoor temperatures without using electricity. Earth tubes should be installed deep enough (typically 6-10 feet underground) to benefit from the earth's stable temperature.

Earth-Sheltered Homes: Building homes partially underground or using bermed earth walls can significantly reduce the impact of external temperature fluctuations. Earth-sheltered homes are naturally cooler in summer due to the thermal mass effect of the surrounding soil, which absorbs and retains heat slowly.

Basement and Cellar Use: For existing homes, basements and cellars can serve as naturally cooler spaces during hot periods. By designing living or working areas below ground level, you can reduce the need for additional cooling systems.

Night Cooling: Utilizing Cooler Nighttime Air

Nighttime Ventilation: Open windows and ventilation panels during the cooler night hours to allow cool air to circulate throughout the home. Thermal chimneys can enhance this process by creating a draft that pulls warm air out as cool air flows in.

Shading and Insulation During the Day: To maximize the effects of night cooling, close windows and cover them with thermal blinds or insulated curtains during the day. This traps the cool air from the night and minimizes heat gain from the sun.

Evaporative Cooling Techniques: In arid climates, using evaporative coolers or swamp coolers can lower temperatures effectively. These devices use water to cool air as it passes through, taking advantage of the dry environment. Solar-powered evaporative coolers are ideal for off-grid settings, providing efficient cooling without external power.

Maintaining Indoor Climate Control Efficiently

Keeping indoor temperatures consistent throughout the year requires proper maintenance and a combination of passive and active techniques tailored to your specific environment.

Seasonal Adjustments for Temperature Control:

Winterization: Prepare for winter by sealing gaps around windows and doors with weather stripping and caulking. Install storm windows or insulated panels to add an extra layer of protection against the cold. Using removable shutters or panels on the outside of the windows can block cold drafts while allowing sunlight in during the day.

Summer Cooling Preparations: Ensure that all ventilation systems, including ceiling and attic fans, are operational before the hot season begins. Clean and inspect earth tubes or other underground cooling systems to make sure they are unobstructed.

Thermal Mass and Energy Storage Techniques:

Storing Heat with Thermal Mass: Use materials like stone, brick, or water barrels inside the home to absorb heat during the day and release it at night. For passive solar systems, these elements can be positioned near windows to capture sunlight effectively.

Using Water as a Thermal Battery: Large water containers can be used as thermal batteries to store coolness or warmth, depending on the season. Place these containers in shaded areas during summer and in sunlit spots during winter to take advantage of their thermal properties.

Monitoring and Automation for Efficient Climate Control:

Thermostats and Monitors: Install manual or solar-powered thermostats to monitor indoor temperatures. Knowing when to open or close vents, windows, or shutters based on temperature readings allows for precise management of indoor climate control.

Automated Systems: For those who prefer a more automated approach, install smart vents or solar-powered actuators that automatically open and close vents or shutters based on temperature sensors. These systems can optimize natural ventilation and maximize passive heating or cooling without manual intervention.

Backup and Redundancy Planning for Extreme Conditions:

Emergency Heating Solutions: In regions prone to extreme cold, maintain a backup heating system, such as propane heaters or kerosene stoves, that can be activated quickly if the primary system fails. Ensure that these are stored safely and are fully operational before the onset of winter.

Cooling Backup for Extreme Heat: For hot climates, a backup plan might include portable battery-operated fans or evaporative cooling units that can provide relief during heatwaves. Ensure batteries are charged and water supplies for evaporative systems are readily available.

Integrating Heating and Cooling Systems with Other Off-Grid Infrastructure

Linking your climate control systems with other off-grid systems, such as water, energy, and insulation, creates a cohesive and efficient homestead setup.

Integrating Solar Power with Heating and Cooling Systems:

Solar Thermal Heating: Install solar panels that not only generate electricity but also heat water for radiators or underfloor heating systems. This integration reduces the need for external fuels and maximizes the efficiency of your solar setup.

Solar-Powered Fans and Ventilation Systems: Use solar panels to power fans that enhance ventilation during summer months. By linking fans and other ventilation equipment directly to solar power, you ensure they operate at peak capacity during the hottest parts of the day when they are most needed.

Maximizing Efficiency with Water and Thermal Systems:

Using Greywater for Cooling: Divert greywater systems to cooling features like ponds or garden beds. The evaporative effect of water on surfaces helps lower surrounding air temperatures, creating a natural cooling zone around the home.

Water-Based Radiant Heating Systems: Connect your solar water heating system to radiant floor or wall systems. These systems distribute heat evenly and use less energy compared to traditional heating methods, improving overall efficiency.

Adapting Insulation Based on Seasonal Needs:

Modular Insulation Panels: Design modular insulation panels that can be added or removed seasonally. For example, thick wool or straw panels can be installed in winter and removed in summer to improve ventilation.

Living Walls and Green Roofs: Plant living walls or green roofs, which provide insulation and help regulate temperatures naturally. Green roofs absorb sunlight and reduce heat gain, while living walls act as insulative barriers and provide shade.

Long-Term Planning and Maintenance for Climate Control Systems

Planning for the long-term success of your off-grid climate control systems involves regular inspections, updates, and contingency planning for extreme weather events.

Regular Maintenance of Systems and Insulation:

Conduct seasonal inspections of heating systems, including checking for leaks in wood stoves, inspecting propane lines, and cleaning solar panels. Maintain insulation by repairing any gaps or damage caused by seasonal expansion and contraction.

Clean and maintain ventilation systems, ensuring that all ducts and vents remain clear of debris and that any automated components are functioning properly.

Upgrading Systems and Integrating New Technologies:

As new technologies become available, explore upgrading existing systems, such as adding solar-powered automated blinds or incorporating phase-change materials (PCM) in walls for improved thermal management.

Expand passive solar capabilities by adding reflective window films or seasonal shading devices that enhance temperature control based on the sun's angle throughout the year.

Emergency Preparedness for Extreme Weather Events:

Keep an emergency stock of fuel sources (wood, propane, batteries) and extra insulation materials to respond quickly to unexpected weather changes. Monitor weather forecasts and prepare the home by sealing windows or deploying emergency heating solutions when needed.

Install storm shutters or reinforced panels for windows and doors to protect against high winds and severe storms, ensuring that the home remains safe and maintains temperature control even in extreme conditions.

Conclusion: Efficiently Managing Off-Grid Heating and Cooling

Maintaining a comfortable off-grid home involves a combination of passive and active methods for heating and cooling. By using sustainable and natural resources like wood stoves, passive solar designs, and earth-cooling systems, you can create an efficient and resilient climate control setup. Incorporating strategic insulation and ventilation practices enhances these systems, ensuring that your home stays comfortable year-round. With proper maintenance and planning for extreme weather events, your off-grid heating and cooling methods can remain efficient and effective for years to come.

In the next chapter, we'll explore off-grid lighting solutions, focusing on how to design and implement energy-efficient lighting using solar, LED systems, and other renewable sources.

Chapter 18: Foraging for Wild Edibles and Medicinal Plants

Foraging for wild edibles and medicinal plants is an essential skill for off-grid living. It not only provides a source of fresh, nutrient-rich food but also offers medicinal remedies that can be critical in remote areas. This chapter covers how to identify edible plants and mushrooms across various regions, gather and use medicinal herbs for basic first aid, and create a forager's calendar to optimize seasonal harvesting.

Identifying Edible Plants and Mushrooms in Different Regions

Learning to recognize and harvest wild edibles safely requires knowledge of local ecosystems and an understanding of which plants are edible and which are potentially harmful. This section outlines common edible plants and mushrooms found in various regions, offering tips for safe and sustainable foraging.

Foraging in Forested Areas:

Berries: Forests often offer a variety of edible berries, such as blackberries, raspberries, blueberries, and elderberries. These fruits are rich in vitamins and antioxidants, making them a valuable food source. When foraging berries, ensure they are ripe and avoid any that have milky sap or a bitter taste, as these may indicate toxicity.

Nuts and Seeds: In temperate forests, look for acorns (from oak trees), hazelnuts, and walnuts. These provide healthy fats and protein. Acorns require processing to remove tannins; soaking and boiling are common methods.

Mushrooms: Edible mushrooms like chanterelles, morels, and porcini can be found in forests, but mushroom identification requires care. Learn to identify key features such as gill patterns, spore prints, and habitat preferences. Avoid mushrooms with white gills, a volva, or a ring, as these characteristics are common in toxic varieties like Amanita.

Foraging in Meadows and Grasslands:

Dandelion (Taraxacum officinale): Dandelions are abundant and entirely edible. Leaves can be used in salads, flowers for tea or wine, and roots roasted for a coffee substitute. Dandelions are high in vitamins A and C, and they are known for their diuretic properties.

Plantain (Plantago major): A common herb found in grassy areas, plantain leaves are edible when young and can be used in salads or cooked like spinach. The leaves also have medicinal uses for treating cuts, bites, and rashes.

Wild Carrot (Daucus carota): Also known as Queen Anne's Lace, the root is edible when young. However, be cautious when identifying this plant, as it closely resembles the poisonous hemlock. The key difference is the hairy stem of the wild carrot, which hemlock lacks.

Foraging in Wetlands and Riverbanks:

Cattails (Typha): Cattails are known as the "supermarket of the wild" because almost every part is edible. The shoots can be eaten raw or cooked, the roots can be dried and ground into flour, and the pollen can be used as a protein-rich supplement.

Watercress (Nasturtium officinale): Found near streams and ponds, watercress is a peppery green that can be used in salads or soups. Ensure that the water source is clean, as watercress absorbs contaminants from its environment.

Wild Mint (Mentha): Mint grows in moist areas and is easily identifiable by its square stem and aromatic leaves. It can be used for teas, flavoring dishes, and medicinal purposes such as soothing digestive issues.

Desert and Arid Region Foraging:

Prickly Pear Cactus (Opuntia): Both the fruit (tuna) and pads (nopales) are edible. The fruit can be eaten raw or juiced, while the pads can be grilled. Be cautious of spines when harvesting.

Mesquite Pods: In desert regions, mesquite trees produce pods that can be ground into flour. This flour is gluten-free and has a sweet, nutty flavor, ideal for baking.

Agave: The hearts of agave plants can be roasted for a sweet, nutritious treat. Agave nectar is also used as a natural sweetener. Ensure proper identification, as some agave species have sharp spines and toxic sap.

Gathering and Using Medicinal Herbs for Basic First Aid

In addition to providing food, many wild plants have medicinal properties. Knowing which herbs to gather and how to use them for basic first aid can be invaluable for off-grid homesteaders.

Calendula (Calendula officinalis):

Uses: Calendula flowers are used for their anti-inflammatory and antiseptic properties. They can be made into salves or teas to treat minor cuts, scrapes, and skin irritations.

Identification: This plant features bright orange or yellow flowers with a mild, pleasant scent. Calendula is often found in meadows and open areas.

Application: Harvest the flowers and dry them for later use. Infuse dried flowers in oil to create a healing salve or brew them for a skin-soothing tea.

Yarrow (Achillea millefolium):

Uses: Yarrow is a powerful astringent that stops bleeding and promotes wound healing. It also has anti-inflammatory properties and can be used as a tea for fevers.

Identification: Yarrow has fern-like leaves and clusters of small white or pink flowers. It grows in a variety of environments, from meadows to forest edges.

Application: Crush fresh yarrow leaves and apply them directly to wounds to stop bleeding. Dried yarrow can be brewed into tea for colds and fevers.

Plantain (Plantago major):

Uses: This versatile plant is effective for treating insect bites, stings, and small cuts. Its leaves contain compounds that reduce swelling and promote healing.

Identification: Plantain has broad leaves with parallel veins and grows low to the ground. It is common in lawns, fields, and roadsides.

Application: Crush fresh leaves and apply them as a poultice to bites and stings. Alternatively, prepare an infusion or tincture for skin applications.

St. John's Wort (Hypericum perforatum):

Uses: Known for its mood-enhancing properties, St. John's Wort is also used to treat burns, bruises, and nerve pain. It has anti-inflammatory and antiviral effects.

Identification: This plant features yellow flowers with tiny black dots on the petals and grows in open fields and along roadsides.

Application: Create an oil infusion with the flowers for topical use on burns and bruises. For mood support, dried flowers can be brewed into tea, but consult a healthcare professional before internal use due to possible interactions with medications.

Burdock (Arctium lappa):

Uses: Burdock roots are traditionally used for detoxification and skin conditions such as eczema and acne. Leaves can also be applied to wounds as a poultice.

Identification: Burdock has large, broad leaves and purple thistle-like flowers. It is commonly found in disturbed soils and forest edges.

Application: Harvest roots in the fall, dry them, and use them in decoctions for detoxification. The leaves can be applied fresh to wounds.

Echinacea (Echinacea purpurea):

Uses: Echinacea boosts the immune system and is effective for treating colds and infections. It can also be used topically for wounds and insect bites.

Identification: This plant has tall stems with purple cone-shaped flowers. It grows in prairies and meadows.

Application: Harvest the roots or flowers and dry them for teas and tinctures. Fresh leaves and flowers can be applied to wounds to reduce swelling and promote healing.

Creating a Forager's Calendar for Seasonal Harvesting

Understanding when to harvest different plants and mushrooms ensures that you can gather resources at their peak and plan your foraging activities throughout the year. Creating a forager's calendar helps keep track of seasonal availability.

Spring Foraging (March - May):

Wild Greens: Early spring is ideal for gathering tender wild greens like dandelion, nettles, and ramps (wild leeks). These are nutrient-rich and can be used in salads, soups, or teas.

Medicinal Plants: Look for violets and chickweed, both of which have edible and medicinal properties. Violets are used for respiratory support, while chickweed is anti-inflammatory.

Mushrooms: Morels appear in the spring, especially in moist, shaded areas near hardwood trees. They are a delicacy but require proper identification to avoid toxic lookalikes.

Summer Foraging (June - August):

Berries: Summer is the peak season for wild berries like strawberries, blueberries, raspberries, and blackberries. Harvest these fruits when fully ripe, and consider drying or freezing them for later use.

Flowers and Herbs: Harvest calendula, yarrow, echinacea, and St. John's Wort during summer when their flowers are in bloom. Dry them for use in teas, tinctures, and salves.

Wild Vegetables: Cattail shoots, wild asparagus, and purslane are plentiful in summer. Collect these plants for fresh, nutritious additions to meals.

Fall Foraging (September - November):

Nuts and Seeds: Fall is the time to gather acorns, walnuts, and hazelnuts. Dry and store them for protein-rich snacks or grind into flour for baking.

Roots and Tubers: Dig up roots like burdock and wild carrots in the fall, when they are most nutritious. These roots can be dried and stored for use in soups and teas.

Mushrooms: Fall is another prime season for mushrooms, such as chanterelles, oyster mushrooms, and lion's mane. Always ensure proper identification before consuming any wild mushrooms.

Winter Foraging (December - February):

Evergreens: Pine, spruce, and fir trees offer edible needles that can be used for tea rich in vitamin C. Pine nuts can also be collected during the winter.

Bark and Inner Tree Layers: In survival situations, the inner bark (cambium) of trees like birch and pine can be harvested and eaten. This practice should be done sparingly to avoid damaging trees.

Storage and Preservation: During winter, focus on preserving previously harvested items, such as drying herbs or storing berries in airtight containers. Winter is also a good time to prepare salves and tinctures from dried summer herbs.

Sustainable Foraging Practices

While foraging is a valuable skill, it's essential to practice sustainable harvesting techniques to preserve plant populations and ecosystems for the future.

Harvesting with Care:

Follow the "rule of thirds": take only one-third of any given plant or patch to ensure that it can continue growing and reproduce. Avoid over-harvesting sensitive or rare species.

When gathering roots, dig carefully and re-cover the soil to minimize disturbance. For perennial plants, try to harvest parts of the plant (like leaves or flowers) without uprooting the entire organism.

Avoiding Contaminated Areas:

Forage away from roadsides, industrial sites, or areas with heavy pesticide use, as plants and mushrooms can absorb harmful chemicals. Prioritize wild areas and protected forests where the ecosystem remains undisturbed.

Always wash edible plants thoroughly before consuming, especially if they were gathered near agricultural or urban areas.

Using Foraging Tools Properly:

Carry a foraging knife and small basket or bag for collecting plants without damaging them. Avoid plastic bags, as they can cause plants to wilt quickly.

A field guide specific to your region is an invaluable tool for ensuring proper identification and understanding the ecological role of different plants.

Conclusion: Building Your Foraging Skills for Off-Grid Living

Foraging is not just about gathering food; it's about building a deep connection with your environment and gaining a thorough understanding of the natural resources around you. By learning to identify edible and medicinal plants, creating a seasonal foraging calendar, and practicing sustainable harvesting techniques, you develop a valuable skill set that enhances self-sufficiency and enriches your off-grid lifestyle.

In the next chapter, we'll explore off-grid waste management solutions, focusing on composting toilets, greywater systems, and how to safely dispose of household waste while maintaining environmental integrity.

Chapter 19: Hunting, Fishing, and Trapping for Protein

Off-grid living often requires self-sufficient methods for obtaining protein-rich food sources. Hunting, fishing, and trapping are traditional ways to secure meat, fish, and other animal-based foods, but they require specific skills, knowledge of local ecosystems, and adherence to safety and regulations. In this chapter, we cover basic techniques for hunting small and large game, setting up fishing and trapping systems, and important safety considerations to ensure sustainable and legal practices.

Basic Techniques for Hunting Small and Large Game

Hunting can provide a steady source of protein, but it requires understanding the habits of animals, proper techniques, and the use of appropriate equipment. Below are essential strategies for hunting different types of game.

Hunting Small Game (Rabbits, Squirrels, and Birds):

Choosing the Right Weapon: Small game hunting is typically done with air rifles, small-caliber firearms (.22 rifles), or slingshots. Air rifles are quiet and efficient for close-range hunting, while .22 rifles offer more range and precision.

Tracking and Setting Up: Learn to recognize small game habitats, such as burrows, nests, or areas with abundant food sources like berry bushes or nut trees. Early morning and late afternoon are the best times to hunt, as small animals are most active during these periods.

Snares and Traps: Setting snares or small traps is an effective way to catch small game without expending much energy. Simple wire snares can be placed at the entrance of burrows or in trails frequently used by animals. Ensure the snares are well-hidden and positioned at head height for the specific animal.

Hunting Large Game (Deer, Elk, and Wild Boar):

Selecting the Proper Weapon: For large game, rifles (e.g., .30-06 or .308 calibers) and bows are commonly used. Bows are quieter and may be preferable in areas where stealth is important. Rifles, however, offer more range and power, making them suitable for open terrain or large animals like elk.

Scouting and Stalking: Success in hunting large game depends on scouting the area for signs like tracks, scrapes, and rubs (where animals rub their antlers on trees). Learning to move quietly and stay downwind of your prey is crucial to avoid detection.

Tree Stands and Ground Blinds: Using a tree stand or ground blind can improve your chances of success by giving you a vantage point and concealing your scent. Position these setups near water sources or feeding areas where deer and other game are likely to gather.

Hunting Strategies Based on Seasons:

Deer Hunting: Deer are most active during the rutting season (mating season), which varies by region but typically occurs in the fall. During this time, bucks are more likely to move around in search of does, making them easier to spot. Pay attention to scrapes (bare patches of ground where bucks mark their territory) and set up stands nearby.

Bird Hunting: For bird hunting (e.g., grouse, pheasant, or turkey), timing is crucial. Early mornings and late afternoons are prime hunting times. Use bird calls to attract your target and camouflage to blend in with your surroundings.

Predator Management: In some regions, hunting predators like coyotes or feral hogs is encouraged to manage their populations. This can provide additional meat sources while helping balance the ecosystem.

Setting Up Fishing and Trapping Systems for Food

Fishing and trapping are excellent ways to secure protein with minimal effort once the systems are in place. They offer consistent and renewable food sources if managed properly.

Basic Fishing Techniques:

Hand Line Fishing: This is the simplest method for off-grid fishing. It involves using a fishing line with a hook, sinker, and bait. Hand line fishing is effective for catching small to medium-sized fish in rivers, lakes, or the ocean. Baits like worms, insects, or small pieces of meat work well.

Fishing Rods and Nets: Having a basic fishing rod increases your reach and flexibility, allowing you to cast farther and access deeper water. For larger catches or group fishing, gill nets or cast nets can be effective, but these methods may require permits in certain areas.

Fishing with Traps: Fish traps, such as basket traps or funnel traps, are ideal for passive fishing. These traps guide fish into an enclosure where they cannot escape. Set traps in slow-moving water or tidal areas for the best results, and check them regularly.

Constructing Simple Fish Traps:

Building a Basket Trap: Use woven branches or reeds to construct a basket with a narrow entrance. Place bait inside and submerge the trap in a shallow area where fish congregate. The narrow entrance allows fish to enter but makes it difficult for them to exit.

Rock Weir Traps: Rock weirs are natural fish traps that can be built using rocks arranged in a V-shape in shallow water. The narrow end of the V points downstream, guiding fish into a small holding area where they can be easily caught. Rock weirs are low-maintenance and work well in rivers and streams.

Trapping Small Animals for Protein:

Building Simple Snares: Snares are effective for trapping small game like rabbits, squirrels, or birds. Construct a snare using thin wire or cordage fashioned into a loop. Place the snare on a well-used animal trail or near burrows, and ensure it is positioned at the correct height (usually just above ground level for rabbits).

Box Traps and Deadfall Traps: Box traps and deadfall traps are useful for catching animals like raccoons or ground-dwelling birds. A box trap uses a simple bait mechanism to lure animals inside, while a deadfall trap relies on a heavy object that falls when triggered. These traps are effective but require precise construction to ensure they function correctly and humanely.

Water Traps for Muskrats and Beavers: In areas with abundant waterways, water traps can target animals like muskrats or beavers. Conibear traps are commonly used for these species, but they must be set properly in water channels or burrows. Always follow local regulations when trapping in water to ensure compliance.

Setting Up a Long-Term Trapping System:

Create a trap line, a series of strategically placed traps along a trail or in an area known for animal activity. A well-organized trap line can provide a steady food supply with minimal effort once established. Check traps regularly, not only for humane reasons but also to maintain the efficiency of the setup.

Rotate trap locations to prevent animals from becoming accustomed to them. Overuse in one area may decrease effectiveness as animals learn to avoid traps.

Safety Considerations and Regulations for Hunting and Fishing

Engaging in hunting, fishing, and trapping activities requires awareness of safety protocols and adherence to local laws and regulations. This ensures that you harvest resources sustainably and minimize risks to yourself and others.

Firearm Safety and Regulations:

Always follow basic firearm safety principles, including treating every gun as if it is loaded, keeping your finger off the trigger until ready to shoot, and being aware of your target and what lies beyond it. Consider taking a hunter safety course to learn proper techniques and regulations in your area.

Understand and comply with local hunting seasons and game limits. Regulations vary depending on the species and region, and hunting outside of these guidelines can result in fines or loss of hunting privileges. Many areas require hunting licenses or tags for specific game, so ensure you are legally permitted to hunt before starting.

Fishing and Trapping Regulations:

Fishing regulations, including catch limits and protected species, must be adhered to. Research local guidelines for the specific body of water where you plan to fish, as regulations often vary by season and species. Obtain any necessary fishing licenses or permits before casting your line.

For trapping, many regions require trapper education courses and permits to ensure humane and sustainable practices. Trapping laws also regulate the types of traps that can be used and the species that can be targeted. Understanding these rules is essential to avoid penalties and protect wildlife populations.

Wilderness Survival Safety:

When hunting or trapping, always carry a basic survival kit that includes first aid supplies, a compass, a knife, and fire-starting tools. Knowing how to navigate your surroundings is crucial, especially if you venture into remote areas.

Wear appropriate camouflage or blaze orange gear as required by local regulations. Blaze orange is important during hunting seasons to make yourself visible to other hunters, reducing the risk of accidental shootings.

Environmental and Ethical Considerations:

Practice sustainable and ethical hunting and trapping by respecting wildlife populations and ecosystems. Avoid over-harvesting any species, and target animals that are abundant in the area. If an animal is not harvested ethically (e.g., not killed instantly), be prepared to track and dispatch it humanely.

Avoid disturbing sensitive habitats, such as nesting sites or animal dens, to protect wildlife and maintain healthy ecosystems. Following the "leave no trace" principles ensures that you minimize your impact on the environment while foraging for food.

Improving Skills and Adapting Techniques

Mastering hunting, fishing, and trapping requires ongoing learning and adaptation. Improve your skills by practicing regularly and learning from experienced hunters and foragers.

Tracking and Animal Behavior:

Develop your ability to read tracks, scat, and animal behavior. Identifying animal trails, feeding areas, and bedding sites increases your chances of a successful hunt. Practice identifying these signs in different environments to expand your knowledge base.

Familiarize yourself with the calls and sounds of various animals. Learning to mimic these sounds, such as turkey calls or duck calls, can help attract game during hunts.

Improving Marksmanship and Accuracy:

Regular practice with your chosen hunting equipment (e.g., bow, rifle) is essential. Practice shooting at various distances and in different conditions to simulate real-life scenarios. Shooting from elevated positions or while in motion improves your adaptability.

Invest in quality optics, such as scopes or binoculars, to improve accuracy. Ensuring you can accurately identify and aim at your target minimizes the risk of wounding animals and improves overall hunting success.

Enhancing Fishing Techniques:

Experiment with different lures, baits, and fishing techniques to determine what works best in your area. Fish behavior changes with seasons, so understanding when and where certain species are most active can make a significant difference.

Practice catch-and-release techniques when targeting non-essential species or when reaching daily limits to maintain fish populations. Handling fish gently and using barbless hooks helps reduce injury and mortality rates.

Learning from Local Knowledge and Experts:

Connect with local hunters, fishers, and trappers who have extensive knowledge of the area. Their insights on animal habits, local regulations, and techniques can be invaluable. Participating in community hunts or group fishing expeditions is also an excellent way to learn.

Explore online resources, books, and survival courses that specialize in hunting, fishing, and trapping. Expanding your knowledge base helps you adapt techniques to different regions and conditions, ensuring a successful off-grid protein supply.

Sustainable Harvesting and Managing Wildlife Populations

Sustainable practices are crucial for maintaining wildlife populations and ensuring future hunting and fishing opportunities. Respecting animal populations and the environment allows for long-term use of these resources.

Rotating Hunting Areas:

Avoid hunting the same area repeatedly, as this can lead to over-harvesting and disrupt local wildlife patterns. Rotate hunting spots and trap lines to minimize impact and allow animal populations to recover.

Follow local wildlife conservation guidelines that monitor and manage populations. Many areas set quotas or limits based on population studies to prevent species depletion.

Using All Parts of the Animal:

Respect animals by utilizing as much of the harvested animal as possible. For large game, process the meat efficiently and use bones for tools or broth. Pelts can be tanned for clothing or trading, and sinew can be used for cordage.

Learn to field-dress and process animals efficiently to avoid spoilage, especially in warm climates. Proper knowledge of butchering techniques ensures the meat remains safe and usable.

Managing Fish and Water Resources:

Rotate fishing locations to avoid depleting fish populations in a single area. Practice catch limits and seasonal fishing to align with breeding patterns, ensuring that fish have time to spawn and repopulate.

Avoid polluting waterways by using biodegradable bait and avoiding plastic or metal materials that can harm aquatic ecosystems. Respect buffer zones and protected areas that are vital for fish breeding and biodiversity.

Understanding Ecosystem Interactions:

Hunting and trapping affect more than just the targeted species. Be mindful of the predator-prey balance and how removing certain animals impacts the broader ecosystem. For example, reducing predator populations can lead to overpopulation of certain species, affecting plant life and other animals.

Participate in conservation programs or efforts that work to manage and protect wildlife habitats. These programs often provide opportunities to contribute positively to ecosystem health while practicing sustainable hunting and fishing techniques.

Adapting Hunting and Fishing Techniques for Different Climates and Regions

Adapting to various environments and climates is crucial for successful off-grid hunting and fishing. Techniques that work in one region may need modification when applied elsewhere.

Cold Climate Techniques:

In colder regions, ice fishing provides access to fish even when lakes are frozen. Set up ice shanties or shelters over holes drilled in the ice. Use bait suited to cold-water fish species like trout or perch.

For hunting in snowy conditions, invest in insulated clothing and learn to identify tracks in the snow. Snow also helps camouflage footprints and scent, allowing for stealthier approaches to prey.

Desert and Arid Region Techniques:

Hunting in desert environments requires hydration strategies and understanding of water sources. Animals in these regions often gather near waterholes or oases. Set up blinds or observation points near these resources.

Fishing in desert regions might involve targeting oases or reservoirs. Understanding local fish species and their behavior during different times of day is key to success.

Coastal and Wetland Techniques:

In coastal areas, use techniques like crabbing and spearfishing. Tides play a crucial role, so timing is essential when setting nets or casting lines. Tide pools and shallow waters often host edible shellfish like clams or mussels.

Wetlands offer opportunities for duck hunting and trapping water-based animals like muskrats or beavers. Employ water-resistant gear and camouflaged clothing suited for the wet environment.

Conclusion: Building Sustainable Protein Systems Off-Grid

Hunting, fishing, and trapping are vital skills for off-grid survival, providing essential protein sources that can be adapted to various environments and climates. By learning proper techniques, understanding regulations, and respecting wildlife and ecosystems, you can develop a sustainable food system that enhances your self-sufficiency. Through regular practice and adapting to the specific challenges of your region, these methods can support your homestead for years to come.

In the next chapter, we will explore crafting and maintaining essential tools, focusing on creating durable and effective tools for hunting, trapping, and daily use on the homestead.

Chapter 20: Managing Off-Grid Safety and Emergency Preparedness

Living off-grid offers independence and self-sufficiency but also comes with its own set of risks. Natural disasters, unexpected events, and encounters with wildlife can all pose significant challenges. Being prepared with the right strategies and tools is essential for ensuring the safety of yourself and your homestead. This chapter covers how to prepare for natural disasters and emergencies, implement self-defense and wildlife management strategies, and build a comprehensive emergency survival kit to keep you protected in critical situations.

Preparing for Natural Disasters and Unexpected Events

When living off-grid, it's important to anticipate and prepare for natural disasters that are common to your area, whether it's extreme weather, wildfires, earthquakes, or flooding. Proper planning and having the necessary supplies in place can make all the difference.

Assessing Risks Based on Location:

Research Local Hazards: Understand the natural disaster risks specific to your region, such as hurricanes in coastal areas, wildfires in forested zones, or tornadoes in plains regions. Consider historical weather patterns and consult local resources or government agencies to identify potential threats.

Mapping Evacuation Routes: Plan multiple evacuation routes in case one is blocked by a disaster. Practice these routes regularly with family members to ensure familiarity. If possible, establish a safe meeting point at a neighbor's homestead or a nearby town.

Creating a Disaster Preparedness Plan:

Communication Plan: Establish a communication system with family members or nearby neighbors. Consider using two-way radios or solar-powered emergency radios to stay informed when cell service may be unavailable.

Weather Monitoring: Install a weather alert system on your homestead, such as a battery-operated or solar-powered radio that receives NOAA weather updates. Stay informed about severe weather threats and prepare accordingly.

Reinforcing Structures: To prepare for high winds, earthquakes, or heavy snow, reinforce buildings with braces, storm shutters, and roof anchors. Ensure that your structures are built to withstand local weather conditions.

Stocking and Storing Emergency Supplies:

Store at least two weeks' worth of non-perishable food and water for each person. Canned goods, dried beans, rice, and freeze-dried meals are suitable options. Keep water stored in sealed containers or barrels and rotate supplies regularly.

Backup Power and Lighting: Have a solar generator, wind turbine, or battery bank for emergency power. Solar-powered lights and hand-crank flashlights are also essential for maintaining visibility during outages.

Specific Preparations for Common Natural Disasters:

Wildfires: In fire-prone areas, create a defensible space around your home by clearing brush, trimming trees, and keeping woodpiles away from structures. Install fire-resistant barriers such as gravel or stone paths and use metal roofing to reduce fire risks. Have a fire extinguisher and water hoses accessible at all times.

Flooding: For homesteads in flood zones, elevate critical structures like storage sheds, battery banks, and food supplies. Use sandbags around entry points and maintain clear drainage systems to divert water away from your living areas.

Earthquakes: Secure heavy items like shelves, water tanks, and solar panels to prevent them from shifting or falling. Use straps or brackets designed to withstand seismic activity and ensure emergency supplies are easily accessible.

Self-Defense Strategies and Wildlife Management

In remote areas, both human and wildlife encounters may pose risks. Establishing self-defense measures and managing wildlife effectively are key to maintaining safety.

Personal Self-Defense:

Firearms Training: If legally permissible and practical for your area, firearms can provide essential protection. Take a firearms safety course to learn proper handling, storage, and usage. Ensure firearms are stored securely in a locked cabinet or safe, with ammunition stored separately.

Non-Lethal Defense Tools: Consider carrying non-lethal tools like pepper spray, stun guns, or batons for self-defense. These can be effective for deterring threats without causing permanent harm.

Self-Defense Training: Basic self-defense courses can teach techniques for fending off attackers or managing physical confrontations. Practicing these skills ensures confidence and preparedness during unexpected encounters.

Wildlife Management:

Understanding Local Wildlife: Know the types of wildlife that inhabit your area and their behaviors. Common animals that may pose risks include bears, mountain lions, coyotes, and feral hogs. Learn to recognize their tracks and signs to gauge if they frequent your property.

Animal Deterrents: Install motion-activated lights and noisemakers around the perimeter of your homestead to deter nocturnal wildlife. Fencing is crucial, particularly for protecting livestock and garden areas. Use electric fences where appropriate and maintain them regularly.

Storing Food Securely: Prevent wildlife from being attracted to your homestead by storing food securely in bear-proof containers or elevated food storage boxes. Avoid leaving animal feed, garbage, or compost exposed, as these can attract large predators and pests.

Setting Up a Perimeter Security System:

Cameras and Alarms: Install solar-powered security cameras to monitor activity around your homestead. Motion sensors connected to alarms can alert you to movement at night or when you are away from your primary dwelling.

Guard Animals: Dogs, particularly those bred for guarding, can be valuable in remote areas. Livestock guardian dogs or watchdogs can help protect livestock from predators and alert you to intruders.

Establishing Observation Points: Set up lookout points around your property with a clear line of sight for monitoring wildlife and human activity. These points can also serve as hunting blinds or emergency escape routes if needed.

Building and Storing an Emergency Survival Kit

An emergency survival kit is a crucial element for off-grid safety, providing essential tools and supplies for surviving various situations. A well-stocked kit should cover basic needs such as food, water, shelter, medical supplies, and navigation tools.

Assembling the Core Survival Kit:

Food and Water: Pack high-calorie, non-perishable foods like energy bars, dehydrated meals, and trail mix. Include water purification tablets, a portable water filter, and collapsible water containers to ensure access to clean water.

Shelter and Warmth: Include a compact tent, thermal blanket, and emergency poncho for protection against the elements. Fire-starting tools such as waterproof matches, a ferro rod, and tinder are essential for warmth and cooking.

Navigation and Communication: Carry a compass, map of the local area, and a multi-tool with basic functions (e.g., knife, saw, pliers). A solar-powered emergency radio or two-way radio helps you stay informed and connected.

First Aid Supplies:

Basic Medical Supplies: Assemble a comprehensive first-aid kit that includes bandages, gauze, antiseptics, tweezers, scissors, and adhesive tape. Add medications like pain relievers, antihistamines, and antiseptic ointments.

Advanced First Aid: In remote settings, it's advisable to include advanced items such as tourniquets, hemostatic dressings, and splints for treating severe injuries. Learning basic wilderness first aid or emergency medical response techniques is also crucial.

Wound Care and Trauma Kits: For areas with higher risks of injury (e.g., using tools or firearms), include a trauma kit with items like pressure bandages, chest seals, and burn dressings. These can be life-saving in serious situations where professional medical help may be hours away.

Specialized Tools for Emergency Situations:

Signaling Devices: Include whistles, signal mirrors, and flares to alert rescuers or neighbors in case of emergencies. Ensure they are easily accessible within your survival kit.

Rope and Cordage: Pack at least 50 feet of paracord, which can be used for building shelters, securing gear, or assisting in rescues. Paracord is versatile and compact, making it ideal for emergency use.

Waterproof Bags and Containers: Protect your supplies by using waterproof bags or hard cases. These keep gear dry and functional in wet conditions, especially during floods or storms.

Long-Term Emergency Storage Solutions

For off-grid homesteads, storing emergency supplies in secure, accessible locations is essential for quick response in crises.

Setting Up a Safe Storage Area:

Designate a secure location, such as a basement, bunker, or shed, for storing emergency supplies. Ensure it is well-ventilated, waterproof, and fire-resistant. Keeping the area organized and maintaining an updated inventory helps you manage and rotate supplies efficiently.

Install shelves, storage bins, and emergency lighting to make the space functional and easily accessible during power outages or low visibility.

Backup Shelter and Supplies:

Consider setting up a secondary shelter on your property (e.g., a small cabin or underground bunker) stocked with backup supplies like food, water, medical kits, and clothing. This secondary location can serve as a safe retreat if the main dwelling is compromised due to fire, flooding, or other disasters.

Include a cache of tools (e.g., hatchet, shovel, saw) at the backup shelter to aid in building, repairing, or foraging. Emergency firewood or fuel stored safely ensures you have access to heat during cold weather.

Rotating and Maintaining Emergency Supplies:

Rotate food and water supplies regularly to ensure freshness. Label containers with expiration dates and establish a rotation schedule for canned goods, dehydrated foods, and emergency rations.

Test and maintain emergency tools and equipment, such as fire extinguishers, radios, and solar panels. Performing regular checks ensures that these items will work when needed.

Safety Drills and Emergency Simulations

Practicing safety drills and emergency scenarios can prepare you and your family for quick, effective responses during a crisis.

Simulated Drills:

Organize safety drills that simulate various emergencies such as fire, flooding, wildlife encounters, or medical crises. Drills help ensure everyone knows their role and the fastest way to access supplies, communicate, or evacuate if needed.

For natural disasters like wildfires or hurricanes, practice evacuation routes and shelter-in-place procedures. Time the drills to see how quickly you can respond and identify any weak points that need improvement.

Regular Training and Skill Development:

Take courses in wilderness survival, CPR, and first aid to build a skill set that is applicable in off-grid emergencies. Familiarity with these techniques ensures confidence and competence during high-stress situations.

Engage in firearm safety training if firearms are part of your self-defense plan. Regular practice builds proficiency and reduces risks associated with improper use.

Additional Emergency Considerations for Specific Scenarios

Certain emergencies, like severe injuries or prolonged isolation, require specific strategies and planning. Below are specialized preparedness measures for such situations.

Medical Emergency Response:

In case of severe injuries, have a plan to reach emergency services if possible. Keep a list of nearby clinics or hospitals, and have multiple transportation options available, including ATVs or 4x4 vehicles for rough terrain.

Create an emergency contact list with names and phone numbers of neighbors, local emergency services, and family members. Keep this list in a waterproof container within your survival kit and in your primary shelter.

Extended Isolation and Food Shortages:

In the event of prolonged isolation due to natural disasters or supply chain disruptions, have long-term food storage solutions like freeze-dried meals and canned goods that can sustain your homestead for several months.

Develop self-sufficiency skills such as hunting, foraging, and gardening to supplement food supplies when shortages occur. A well-maintained root cellar or cold storage system can preserve food harvested from the garden for extended periods.

Managing Long-Term Power Outages:

Prepare for extended power outages by having multiple energy sources like solar panels, wind turbines, or hand-crank generators. Ensure batteries and inverters are well-maintained and fully charged.

Use energy-efficient cooking methods such as wood stoves or solar ovens that do not rely on electricity. This ensures that you can prepare food and heat your space without depleting fuel supplies.

Adapting Emergency Preparedness Based on Climate and Terrain

Preparedness strategies must be adapted to suit the specific climate and terrain of your off-grid location, as these factors significantly impact the types of emergencies you may face.

Cold Climate Preparedness:

In colder regions, prioritize winterization of your shelter by insulating walls, floors, and windows. Store ample firewood or alternative heating fuels like propane or kerosene, and maintain all heating systems regularly to ensure functionality.

Prepare for winter storms by stocking extra blankets, insulated clothing, and emergency rations that are high in calories to sustain energy levels during prolonged cold periods.

Desert and Arid Region Preparedness:

For desert environments, focus on water conservation and storage. Install large-capacity rainwater tanks and build shade structures to keep water cool. Store non-perishable, heat-resistant food supplies, as high temperatures can shorten food shelf life.

Establish cooling methods such as earth tubes or solar-powered fans to manage extreme heat. Keep emergency kits stocked with electrolyte solutions to prevent dehydration.

Mountain and Forested Region Preparedness:

In mountainous or forested areas, plan for landslides, heavy snowfall, or wildfire risks. Keep tools like chainsaws, shovels, and fire extinguishers readily available.

Practice setting up firebreaks around your property and maintain defensible space to reduce the risk of fire spreading to structures. Ensure your shelter is built with materials and designs that can withstand heavy snow or high winds common in these regions.

Conclusion: Comprehensive Off-Grid Safety and Preparedness

Managing safety and emergency preparedness off-grid requires a proactive and strategic approach. By understanding the risks associated with your environment, setting up self-defense and wildlife management measures, and building comprehensive emergency kits, you ensure that you are well-prepared for a variety of situations. Regular practice, skill development, and proper maintenance of supplies and equipment are vital to ensuring resilience and adaptability in critical moments.

In the next chapter, we'll explore crafting and maintaining essential tools, focusing on creating durable and effective tools for hunting, trapping, and daily use on the homestead.

Chapter 21: Maintaining and Upgrading Power Systems

Maintaining and upgrading off-grid power systems is crucial for ensuring a consistent energy supply and increasing the efficiency and output of your solar, wind, and hydroelectric setups. Regular maintenance keeps these systems operating effectively, while strategic upgrades can significantly enhance performance, making your off-grid homestead more resilient and self-sufficient. This chapter covers essential maintenance tasks, upgrading equipment for better power output, and troubleshooting common issues associated with off-grid power systems.

Regular Maintenance Tasks for Solar, Wind, and Hydro Systems

Each power system has specific maintenance needs that must be addressed to ensure reliability and longevity. Below are detailed tasks for maintaining solar panels, wind turbines, and hydroelectric setups.

Solar Power Systems:

Panel Cleaning: Dust, dirt, and debris can accumulate on solar panels, reducing their efficiency. Clean panels at least once a month using a soft brush or squeegee with water to remove grime without scratching the surface. Avoid using harsh chemicals that can damage the panels.

Inspecting Connections: Regularly check the wiring and connections between panels, charge controllers, and inverters for signs of corrosion, loose connections, or wear and tear. Tighten connections as needed and replace any damaged wires or connectors to prevent energy loss or shorts.

Battery Maintenance: For systems using lead-acid batteries, check electrolyte levels monthly and top off with distilled water as needed. Monitor for corrosion on battery terminals and clean them with a mixture of baking soda and water to ensure proper conductivity. Lithium-ion batteries require less maintenance but should still be inspected for swelling, leaks, or performance issues.

Monitoring Performance: Use a solar monitoring system to track the efficiency of your panels. These systems provide data on voltage output and power generation, helping you identify any underperformance early.

Wind Turbine Systems:

Blade Inspection and Cleaning: Check turbine blades for cracks, damage, or build-up of dirt. Clean the blades periodically to maintain their aerodynamic efficiency. Tighten bolts and secure fasteners to prevent the blades from coming loose during operation.

Lubricating Moving Parts: Wind turbines have moving components like bearings and shafts that need to be lubricated regularly. Apply high-quality grease to these parts at least every six months to minimize friction and extend the turbine's lifespan.

Tower Stability and Guy Wires: Inspect the tower and guy wires for any signs of wear or stress. Tighten guy wires and replace any frayed or rusted sections. Check the tower base for corrosion or movement, ensuring it remains stable and secure.

Hydro Power Systems:

Intake and Turbine Maintenance: Clear the intake of debris such as leaves, branches, and sediment that can block water flow and reduce efficiency. Clean and inspect the turbine blades for any signs of wear or damage. Regularly check the shaft and bearings, lubricating them to ensure smooth operation.

Piping and Water Flow: Inspect the penstock (the pipe carrying water to the turbine) for leaks, cracks, or obstructions. Regularly flush the system to remove sediment build-up that can impede water flow and reduce power output.

Electrical System Checks: Ensure that wiring and connections from the turbine to the inverter and battery bank are secure and free of corrosion. Test voltage output and monitor any fluctuations that might indicate issues with the turbine or the water flow.

Upgrading Equipment for Increased Efficiency and Power Output

As technology advances, upgrading your power systems can result in greater efficiency and output. The following sections outline how to upgrade solar, wind, and hydro systems to enhance performance.

Solar System Upgrades:

Panel Upgrades: Consider replacing older panels with higher-efficiency models like monocrystalline panels, which have improved output per square foot compared to polycrystalline or older technologies. New panels may also perform better under low-light conditions.

Adding Solar Trackers: Installing solar trackers can significantly increase energy production by allowing panels to follow the sun's movement. Trackers can boost efficiency by up to 30-40%, especially in areas with fluctuating sunlight.

Inverter Upgrades: If your current inverter is outdated or undersized, upgrading to a hybrid inverter can optimize energy conversion and storage. Hybrid inverters are compatible with multiple power sources (e.g., solar, wind, grid backup) and allow for seamless switching between them.

Wind Turbine System Upgrades:

Turbine Blade Replacement: Upgrading to aerodynamically optimized blades can increase a turbine's efficiency. Modern blades are designed with lightweight composite materials that improve speed and reduce noise levels.

Variable-Speed Controllers: Installing variable-speed controllers allows the turbine to adjust blade speed based on wind conditions, maximizing power output during variable wind speeds. These controllers also help protect the turbine in high-wind situations by slowing down or stopping the blades.

Battery and Storage Enhancements: If your wind turbine is part of a hybrid system, consider expanding your battery bank or switching to lithium-ion batteries, which offer better storage capacity and longer lifespans compared to traditional lead-acid batteries.

Hydro System Upgrades:

Turbine Replacement: Replacing older turbines with modern, high-efficiency models can significantly boost output. Pelton wheels and crossflow turbines are commonly used for small-scale hydro systems and are designed to handle varying water flow conditions efficiently.

Automatic Flow Control Valves: Installing automatic flow control valves allows you to adjust water flow to the turbine based on seasonal changes or energy needs, maintaining optimal output and reducing wear on the system.

Improving Penstock Efficiency: Upgrade to larger or smooth-lined penstock pipes to increase water flow and reduce friction losses. This can result in higher water velocity reaching the turbine, translating into improved energy production.

Troubleshooting Common Power System Issues

Understanding how to diagnose and resolve common issues in off-grid power systems is crucial for maintaining a reliable energy supply. Below are typical problems and troubleshooting tips for solar, wind, and hydro systems.

Solar System Issues:

Low Power Output: If your panels are underperforming, check for shading or dirt accumulation. Clean the panels thoroughly and trim any branches or vegetation obstructing sunlight. Monitor the charge controller and inverter settings to ensure they are configured correctly for optimal output.

Battery Not Charging: If the battery bank isn't charging properly, inspect the connections and fuses for any breaks or loose contacts. Test the solar charge controller to verify it's receiving power from the panels and delivering it to the batteries. Faulty charge controllers may need replacement.

Inverter Problems: Inverters can experience overloads or failures due to excessive loads or internal faults. Reset the inverter and reduce the load to see if it resolves the issue. If the problem persists, test the inverter's output with a multimeter to check for consistent voltage.

Wind Turbine System Issues:

Noise and Vibration: Excessive noise or vibration may indicate a problem with the blades or bearings. Check if the blades are damaged, loose, or unbalanced, and tighten or replace them as necessary. Lubricate the bearings and shaft to ensure smooth operation.

Low Power Output in High Winds: If the turbine isn't producing sufficient power during high winds, the issue might be with the yaw mechanism (which aligns the turbine with the wind) or the controller. Inspect the yaw mechanism for obstructions or wear, and test the controller's settings to verify that it adjusts turbine speed properly.

Overheating Issues: Turbines can overheat if running continuously at high speeds. Install a cooling system or consider adding an automatic shut-off mechanism that halts operation during high winds to prevent damage.

Hydro System Issues:

Reduced Water Flow: If water flow to the turbine decreases, inspect the intake for blockages like leaves, sediment, or ice (in colder climates). Clear any obstructions and consider installing a grate or filter to reduce debris build-up.

Voltage Fluctuations: Fluctuations in voltage output can result from inconsistent water flow or issues with the turbine's generator. Test the generator for proper operation and check for loose connections. If fluctuations persist, calibrate or replace the voltage regulator.

Penstock Leaks: A drop in power output might indicate a leak in the penstock. Inspect the entire length of the pipe for visible leaks or weak spots. Seal small cracks with epoxy, and replace sections that show significant wear.

Upgrading Monitoring and Control Systems

Monitoring and control systems play a vital role in optimizing the performance and efficiency of your off-grid power systems. Upgrading these systems allows for better tracking and automated adjustments.

Installing Advanced Monitoring Systems:

Modern monitoring systems connect directly to solar, wind, and hydro setups, providing real-time data on power output, voltage levels, and battery status. These systems often come with smartphone apps, allowing you to monitor and control your power systems remotely.

Smart Charge Controllers: Upgrade to smart charge controllers that offer MPPT (Maximum Power Point Tracking) capabilities. MPPT controllers optimize power collection by adjusting to changing conditions, ensuring that batteries charge efficiently even in varying light or wind conditions.

Automation for Improved Efficiency:

Automate energy management with hybrid inverters or energy management systems that switch between power sources (e.g., wind to solar) based on availability. These systems optimize power usage, ensuring a consistent supply and minimizing reliance on a single source.

Install automated shut-off switches and circuit breakers that activate during system overloads, protecting your equipment from damage. These systems can be programmed to restart once conditions return to normal, maintaining stability without manual intervention.

Battery Management System (BMS) Upgrades:

A BMS monitors battery health, managing charge levels and protecting against overcharging or deep discharging. Upgrading to a smart BMS provides detailed insights into each cell's status, allowing you to identify underperforming batteries and replace them before they compromise the entire system.

Integrating the BMS with your monitoring system ensures that you receive alerts on battery performance, allowing for proactive management and extending the overall lifespan of your battery bank.

Optimizing System Efficiency Through Site-Specific Adjustments

To maximize the efficiency of your power systems, tailor your setup based on specific site conditions like sunlight exposure, wind patterns, and water flow characteristics.

Solar Array Orientation and Angle Adjustments:

Ensure that your solar panels are positioned at the optimal angle based on your geographical location. Adjust the tilt of the panels seasonally (e.g., more vertical in winter and flatter in summer) to maximize sunlight absorption. If using solar trackers, regularly calibrate them to ensure accurate tracking of the sun's movement.

Reduce Shading: Trim nearby trees or adjust panel placement to minimize shading, which can significantly reduce output. For permanent shading issues, consider using microinverters or power optimizers that isolate shaded panels and maximize the output from unshaded ones.

Wind Turbine Placement and Tower Height Adjustments:

Place turbines at optimal heights (typically 30 feet or more above ground level) to capture the strongest and most consistent winds. Avoid placing turbines near obstacles like buildings or tall trees, which can create turbulence and reduce efficiency.

Use anemometers to measure wind speeds at different heights and locations before finalizing tower placement. Adjust tower height or location based on these measurements to maximize energy capture.

Hydro System Flow Optimization:

Analyze water flow patterns to determine the best placement for your intake. Ensure that the intake is located where water flow remains consistent year-round, avoiding areas that may freeze or dry up during certain seasons.

Build diversion channels or intake pools to manage water flow effectively, especially in fluctuating rivers or streams. These additions can stabilize the water supply and maintain turbine efficiency.

Long-Term Maintenance and System Upgrades Planning

For long-term sustainability, create a maintenance schedule and upgrade plan that accounts for wear and changing technology.

Annual System Checkups:

Conduct a thorough inspection of all components, including panels, inverters, turbines, and hydro generators, at least once a year. Test each part for performance and efficiency, and replace aging components before they fail.

Schedule battery testing and rotation (if applicable) to ensure that all batteries remain within their optimal charge capacity. Plan for battery bank replacements every 5-10 years depending on the type of batteries used.

Staying Up-to-Date with Technology:

Stay informed about advancements in renewable energy technology, such as more efficient battery solutions, improved turbine designs, or new solar panel materials. Upgrading periodically can significantly boost efficiency and extend the lifespan of your power systems.

When upgrading, opt for modular systems that allow for future expansions. This flexibility makes it easier to integrate new components or expand your power capacity without overhauling the entire setup.

Building Redundancy into Power Systems:

For greater reliability, consider setting up multiple types of power generation (e.g., combining solar with wind or hydro). Hybrid systems provide backup power options, ensuring that energy continues to flow even if one system underperforms due to weather or mechanical issues.

Maintain a backup generator (propane or diesel) for emergency use. While these are less sustainable long-term, they offer a critical safety net during system failures or extreme weather conditions.

Optimizing Off-Grid Power Efficiency with Energy Conservation Practices

To maximize the benefits of your power systems, pair them with energy-efficient practices and equipment throughout your homestead.

Energy-Efficient Appliances:

Install LED lighting and energy-efficient appliances like solar refrigerators, low-power fans, and water-efficient pumps. These reduce overall power consumption, ensuring that your systems can keep up with demand.

Use timers and sensors for lighting and other energy-consuming devices to automatically turn them off when not needed. This helps reduce waste and conserves power for essential tasks.

Implementing Smart Energy Usage Strategies:

Monitor energy usage patterns and adjust activities to align with peak power generation. For example, run washing machines or charge devices during sunny periods if relying on solar power. This reduces strain on the battery bank and optimizes power use.

Insulate your shelter to maintain indoor temperatures, minimizing the need for heating or cooling systems that draw power. Proper insulation keeps energy demand low and maximizes the efficiency of your off-grid power setup.

Conclusion: Ensuring a Reliable and Efficient Off-Grid Power System

Maintaining and upgrading your off-grid power systems is a continuous process that requires regular monitoring, strategic upgrades, and a proactive approach to troubleshooting. By investing in maintenance and optimizing your equipment, you ensure that your solar, wind, and hydro systems provide consistent and reliable power. Combining these practices with energy conservation strategies maximizes the efficiency of your setup, allowing you to sustain your off-grid lifestyle successfully.

In the next chapter, we will explore essential tool crafting and maintenance, focusing on building durable tools for hunting, trapping, and everyday use on the homestead.

Chapter 22: Expanding Your Homestead: Structures and Outbuildings

Expanding your homestead with essential structures like barns, coops, greenhouses, and storage sheds enhances self-sufficiency, supports animal husbandry, and extends growing seasons. Building these outbuildings sustainably using recycled and natural materials minimizes environmental impact and can reduce costs. This chapter explores how to plan, design, and construct these structures, using practical methods tailored for off-grid homesteads.

Building Barns, Coops, Greenhouses, and Storage Sheds

Barns for Livestock and Storage:

Designing a Multi-Functional Barn: A well-designed barn serves multiple purposes, such as housing livestock, storing feed, and providing shelter for equipment. When building a barn, consider a pole barn structure, which uses posts driven into the ground as the primary support. This design is simple, cost-effective, and adaptable to various sizes and needs.

Ventilation and Insulation: Proper ventilation is crucial for barns, especially for livestock. Incorporate windows, vents, or a cupola to allow for airflow, preventing moisture buildup and maintaining air quality. If your climate requires it, insulate the barn using straw bales or recycled wool insulation to maintain a stable temperature in extreme weather.

Flooring Options: For livestock, use a combination of packed earth, straw bedding, or concrete in high-traffic areas like feeding and milking stations. This ensures durability and easy cleaning. Elevate feed storage areas on wooden platforms to keep supplies dry and safe from rodents.

Chicken Coops and Small Animal Housing:

Modular Coop Designs: Building a modular chicken coop allows you to expand or reconfigure the structure as needed. Incorporate nesting boxes, roosting bars, and ventilation windows to keep chickens healthy. Use a movable coop (tractor coop) design if you want to rotate chickens around different parts of your land for fertilization and pest control.

Predator Protection: To protect chickens from predators, use hardware cloth for fencing instead of standard chicken wire, which is often too weak. Bury the fencing at least 12 inches deep around the perimeter to prevent digging animals from accessing the coop. Include lockable doors to secure the coop at night.

Water and Feed Systems: Install an automatic or gravity-fed water system using rainwater catchment connected to water troughs. This reduces the need for manual filling and ensures a consistent water supply. Feeders can also be set up with PVC pipes to create a simple, gravity-fed distribution system.

Greenhouses for Year-Round Growing:

Choosing the Right Greenhouse Type: Depending on your space and climate, select a greenhouse style that fits your needs. Hoop houses are inexpensive and easy to build, using PVC pipes or metal frames covered with polyethylene sheeting. For more durability and insulation, build a polycarbonate panel greenhouse, which provides better protection against wind and cold.

Passive Solar Heating: Position the greenhouse with a south-facing orientation (in the northern hemisphere) to maximize sunlight exposure. Incorporate thermal mass elements like stone or water barrels that absorb heat during the day and release it at night, stabilizing the temperature inside the greenhouse.

Ventilation and Shade: Install roof vents and side windows to allow for airflow, preventing overheating. Use shade cloths or roll-up sides to regulate temperature during the hottest parts of the day. Automated vent systems, powered by solar energy, can further optimize temperature control.

Storage Sheds for Tools and Supplies:

Simple Shed Construction: Storage sheds are versatile and can be constructed with basic materials like recycled wood pallets, corrugated metal, or even earthbag walls. Earthbag sheds, for example, are highly durable and provide insulation for temperature-sensitive items.

Organizing the Interior: Incorporate adjustable shelving and hanging racks to maximize vertical space, keeping tools, seeds, and supplies organized and accessible. Use clear containers for small items like screws and bolts to make them easy to identify and retrieve.

Security Features: Equip the shed with lockable doors and consider adding a motion-sensor light for security. This deters wildlife and potential intruders while providing light when accessing tools at night.

Using Recycled and Natural Materials for Sustainable Building

Sustainable building practices not only reduce costs but also minimize environmental impact. Using local, recycled, or natural materials is an effective way to construct long-lasting, eco-friendly structures.

Recycled Wood and Metal:

Salvaging Wood: Recycled wood from old barns, pallets, or construction sites can be used for framing, siding, or even flooring. Ensure that the wood is treated for pests and weatherproofed with natural oils like linseed oil.

Metal Roofing and Siding: Corrugated metal sheets from decommissioned buildings are excellent for roofing and siding sheds or barns. Metal provides durability and weather resistance, particularly in areas prone to heavy rain or snow.

Natural Building Materials:

Earthbags and Cob Construction: For long-term, durable structures like storage sheds or animal shelters, earthbags (sandbags filled with soil) or cob (a mix of clay, sand, straw, and water) offer excellent insulation and thermal mass. Earthbag buildings are also earthquake-resistant, making them suitable for areas with seismic activity.

Straw Bales: Straw bale construction is ideal for creating well-insulated walls in greenhouses or barns. Bales are stacked and secured with rebar, then plastered with earthen or lime plaster to protect them from moisture and pests.

Rammed Earth and Stone: For foundations and walls, rammed earth or stone offers both strength and natural thermal regulation. These materials are locally sourced, reducing transportation costs and their environmental footprint.

Recycled Glass and Bottle Walls:

Glass bottles can be incorporated into walls as decorative and functional elements, allowing light to pass through and adding insulation. Bottle walls are constructed by stacking bottles horizontally within a cob or concrete frame.

Windows from Recycled Glass: Use salvaged glass windows or frames from older buildings to reduce costs. These can be fitted into greenhouses, coops, or barns, providing natural light while minimizing waste.

Planning and Implementing New Projects on Your Property

When expanding your homestead, careful planning and phased implementation are key to maximizing efficiency and minimizing disruption. Follow these steps to ensure that new projects are successful and sustainable.

Assessing Needs and Prioritizing Projects:

Identify Essential Structures: Consider which structures are most critical to your homestead's growth, such as a greenhouse to extend the growing season, a barn for livestock, or a storage shed for tools. Prioritize projects based on your immediate needs, available resources, and climate conditions.

Budgeting and Resource Planning: Estimate the cost of materials, tools, and labor for each project. Decide whether you will use recycled materials or purchase new ones, and source local supplies whenever possible to reduce costs. Calculate how long each project will take and allocate time accordingly.

Site Selection and Design Considerations:

Choosing the Best Location: For each structure, select a location that maximizes its functionality. For example, place a chicken coop near your garden so chickens can access and fertilize soil. Position a greenhouse where it gets the most sunlight and is sheltered from strong winds.

Drainage and Terrain: Consider the terrain and soil type when building. Avoid low-lying areas prone to flooding for structures like coops and barns. If building on a slope, ensure that the foundation is leveled, and incorporate drainage channels to divert water away from structures.

Orientation and Sun Exposure: Plan the orientation of each building based on the sun's path. Structures like greenhouses should face south (in the northern hemisphere) for maximum sunlight, while barns and sheds can be positioned to block cold winds from the north.

Phased Implementation for Large Projects:

Breaking Down the Project: Divide large projects into phases, such as site preparation, foundation building, framing, and finishing. This approach allows you to complete stages systematically, ensuring that each phase is properly executed before moving on to the next.

Resource Allocation: Schedule resource delivery and labor based on each phase. For example, order recycled wood and framing materials early in the process, while insulation and interior fixtures can be sourced later.

Building Temporary Structures: If a project will take multiple seasons to complete, consider building temporary structures (e.g., mobile coops, simple hoop houses) to serve your needs in the interim. These can be moved or repurposed once the permanent structures are finished.

Building and Expanding Fencing Systems:

Fencing is essential for protecting livestock, defining garden areas, and securing the perimeter of your homestead. When planning new outbuildings, consider how fences will integrate with these structures.

Types of Fencing: Choose materials that are durable and suitable for your livestock. For example, use electric fencing for larger animals like goats and cattle, and hardware cloth for poultry enclosures. Fences can also be constructed using natural materials like woven willow branches for smaller garden areas.

Expandable Designs: Plan fencing that can be expanded as your homestead grows. Modular fence panels or posts set at regular intervals allow for easy extension when new structures are added.

Integrating Renewable Energy Solutions:

Solar-Powered Systems: Integrate solar panels into your outbuildings to provide power for lights, electric fences, or water pumps. Greenhouses and barns are ideal locations for solar installations due to their roof surface area and exposure to sunlight.

Rainwater Harvesting: Incorporate rainwater harvesting systems into new structures. Adding gutters and downspouts to barns, coops, and sheds allows you to collect and store water for irrigation or animal use. Use storage tanks or barrels connected to drip systems for efficient water management.

Sustainable Landscaping Around New Structures

Creating a sustainable landscape around your new buildings enhances functionality, improves aesthetics, and supports local ecosystems.

Edible Landscaping and Permaculture Design:

Planting Edible Perennials: Surround greenhouses and barns with fruit trees, berry bushes, or herb gardens to create edible landscapes. These plants not only provide food but also help with water retention and soil stabilization.

Swales and Contour Planting: Use swales (shallow ditches) along contours to manage water runoff and irrigate plants naturally. This method is especially useful around garden sheds and greenhouses, directing water to where it's most needed.

Building with Local Biodiversity in Mind:

Plant native shrubs and trees that support local wildlife and create windbreaks for structures like greenhouses and coops. This encourages biodiversity while providing habitats for beneficial insects and pollinators that support your garden.

Creating Pollinator Gardens: Designate areas around greenhouses and storage sheds as pollinator gardens, filled with wildflowers and plants that attract bees and butterflies. This improves pollination rates for your crops and enhances ecological balance on your homestead.

Soil Health and Mulching:

Mulch Pathways and Garden Beds: Use mulch around the foundations of new structures to manage soil erosion and improve moisture retention. Organic mulches like straw or wood chips are particularly effective in garden areas and pathways.

Composting Systems: Position compost bins near outbuildings like barns or chicken coops, where manure and plant waste are easily accessible. Composting enhances soil health and reduces waste, providing a sustainable loop for nutrient recycling.

Innovative Building Techniques and Green Design

Incorporating green building techniques improves the sustainability and efficiency of your homestead expansion.

Passive Solar and Thermal Mass Design:

Utilize passive solar design principles when constructing greenhouses and sheds. Orient buildings to maximize sunlight exposure, and incorporate thermal mass (e.g., concrete floors or stone walls) that absorbs and releases heat, maintaining consistent temperatures without additional energy use.

Earthen or Cob Walls: Earthen walls for sheds and greenhouses provide excellent insulation and are made from locally available materials like clay, sand, and straw. These materials retain heat and create a stable environment for growing and storage.

Using Natural Cooling Techniques:

Green Roofs: Install green roofs on storage sheds or animal housing to provide insulation, reduce stormwater runoff, and create habitat for insects and small animals. Green roofs also help regulate temperatures, keeping buildings cooler in summer and warmer in winter.

Cross Ventilation: Design barns and coops with windows or vents on opposite sides to facilitate natural airflow. This reduces the need for mechanical ventilation systems and helps control humidity levels in animal housing.

Modular and Expandable Building Designs:

Prefabricated Panels: Use modular building panels that are easy to assemble and allow for expansion. Prefabricated panels can be made from recycled wood, metal, or composite materials, offering flexibility for future growth or modifications.

Movable Structures: Consider building portable coops, sheds, or shade structures that can be relocated as your homestead layout evolves. Movable structures provide adaptability, allowing you to optimize land use and adjust to seasonal needs.

Long-Term Planning and Integration of New Projects

Proper planning ensures that the structures and systems you implement today will integrate smoothly into your long-term vision for the homestead.

Developing a Master Plan:

Create a master plan that includes existing and future structures, fencing, gardens, and pathways. Map out where new buildings will be placed, considering the layout of water systems, solar energy, and animal enclosures.

Incorporate natural features like streams, hills, and forests into your plan. This allows for better integration of resources such as water for hydro power, wind exposure for turbines, or trees for building materials and shelter.

Building Partnerships and Resources:

Collaborate with other off-grid homesteaders and local builders who have experience in sustainable construction. Joining homesteading communities or online forums can provide access to resources, advice, and sometimes even recycled materials.

Develop relationships with local suppliers who specialize in natural and recycled building materials. They may offer discounts or trade options, helping reduce costs while supporting your homestead's expansion.

Regular Assessment and Adaptation:

Assess your homestead's growth annually, evaluating how new structures perform and if further expansion is needed. Adjust building plans based on observations of animal behavior, plant growth, and water management efficiency.

Keep a building log documenting materials used, construction methods, and maintenance schedules for each structure. This log becomes a valuable reference for future projects and helps ensure consistency in construction quality.

Conclusion: Sustainable Growth for a Self-Sufficient Homestead

Expanding your homestead with thoughtfully designed structures like barns, coops, greenhouses, and storage sheds enhances your self-sufficiency while allowing for sustainable growth. By using recycled and natural materials, planning efficiently, and integrating renewable energy solutions, you create a resilient and adaptable homestead that supports both your immediate and long-term needs.

In the next chapter, we will discuss off-grid heating and cooling techniques, focusing on wood stoves, passive solar methods, and energy-efficient cooling systems that ensure comfort throughout the year.

Chapter 23: Bartering, Trading, and Building a Community

Living off-grid often requires more than just self-sufficiency; it involves building strong relationships with others who share similar lifestyles and values. Bartering, trading, and establishing connections with other homesteaders and local communities can enhance your resources, skills, and security. By fostering a network of cooperation, you create a support system that not only improves day-to-day life but also provides essential aid during emergencies. This chapter covers strategies for building a community, essential skills and resources for bartering, and how to create a robust support network.

Establishing Connections with Other Homesteaders and Local Communities

A successful off-grid lifestyle thrives when connected to a broader network. Building relationships with other homesteaders and local communities opens up opportunities for knowledge exchange, resource sharing, and mutual support.

Finding and Connecting with Other Homesteaders:

Local Meetups and Events: Attend farmers' markets, homesteading workshops, and community events where like-minded individuals gather. These are ideal places to network, exchange ideas, and form partnerships. Engage in conversations and share your experiences; this fosters trust and opens doors for future collaborations.

Online Communities and Forums: Use online platforms such as social media groups, homesteading forums, or local agriculture networks to connect with others beyond your immediate location. These platforms allow for the exchange of advice, bartering of goods, and even trading skills through virtual classes or meetups.

Establishing Local Cooperative Networks: Work with neighboring homesteads to form a cooperative network. This could involve group purchases of bulk supplies, collaborative workdays for larger projects, or shared resources like tractors and tools.

Building Relationships with Local Farmers and Craftsmen:

Local farmers and craftsmen are often open to bartering and can provide valuable resources like fresh produce, livestock feed, and handmade goods. Visit local farms and introduce yourself, explaining your off-grid setup and what skills or goods you can offer in exchange for their products.

Craftsmanship Exchanges: Many off-grid communities have skilled craftsmen, such as blacksmiths, carpenters, or herbalists. Building relationships with these individuals allows you to trade for or learn valuable skills that can support your homestead, such as tool-making, herbal medicine preparation, or woodworking.

Creating a Local Trading Network:

Establish a trading hub where homesteaders and local producers can meet periodically to exchange goods and services. A monthly or seasonal bartering market encourages community involvement and ensures a steady supply of diverse products and resources.

Create a community directory of skills, goods, and services available within your network. This directory can list what each homestead offers, such as fresh eggs, dairy, carpentry services, or gardening tools, making it easier for people to connect and trade efficiently.

Skills and Resources for Bartering and Trading

To be successful in a barter-based economy, it is important to know which skills and resources are most valuable within your community. Having a range of skills and products to offer increases your bargaining power and ensures you can always find something to trade.

Essential Skills for Bartering:

Carpentry and Building: Skills in building structures, repairing tools, or constructing furniture are always in demand in off-grid communities. Offering carpentry services in exchange for food supplies or equipment can be a highly effective barter strategy.

Animal Husbandry: If you have experience with raising livestock, consider trading services like veterinary care, milking, or hoof trimming for goods such as animal feed or fresh produce. Livestock management is a critical skill that benefits many homesteads, making it a valuable barter asset.

Preservation and Food Preparation: Skills in canning, fermenting, and smoking foods are highly prized, especially for those looking to extend their food supplies. Offering classes or trading preserved goods like jams, pickles, or jerky can create multiple barter opportunities.

Crafts and Artisan Skills:

Blacksmithing: Creating and repairing tools, building hardware for homestead structures, and crafting metalwork are valuable skills in off-grid settings. Offering blacksmithing services in exchange for other tools or raw materials helps maintain a steady supply of necessary items.

Textile and Leather Work: The ability to sew, mend, and craft clothing or leather goods like belts, harnesses, and bags is valuable. Trading handmade items or offering repair services in exchange for livestock, seeds, or equipment is a practical way to support the community.

Herbal Medicine and Natural Remedies: Knowledge of herbalism and the ability to create natural remedies, tinctures, and balms is another valuable skill. Offering medicinal herbs or conducting workshops on herbal preparation can generate barter opportunities and strengthen community ties.

Resources for Bartering:

Fresh Produce and Livestock Products: Eggs, milk, cheese, fruits, vegetables, and honey are consistently sought-after items. These perishable goods can be bartered for non-perishable items or services, like equipment repairs or firewood.

Seeds and Gardening Supplies: Heirloom seeds, compost, and soil amendments are vital resources for other homesteaders, especially those expanding their gardens. Trading seeds or offering compost in exchange for tools or labor helps build a resilient agricultural network.

Firewood and Lumber: In colder regions, firewood is essential. If you have access to timber, consider splitting and trading firewood or offering milling services to exchange for food, livestock, or other essentials.

Offering Skills Training and Knowledge Exchange:

Teaching others is a powerful bartering tool. Offering workshops on practical skills such as solar panel installation, gardening techniques, or animal care not only benefits others but also opens the door to bartering for goods and services in return for education.

Skill Swapping: Engage in skill-swapping with other homesteaders. For example, if you have knowledge of building, you might trade lessons in construction for lessons in herbal medicine or gardening.

Creating a Support Network for Emergencies and Cooperative Efforts

A well-connected community is not only a source of resources and knowledge but also a critical support system in times of crisis. Establishing an organized network ensures that homesteaders can rely on each other during emergencies, from natural disasters to equipment failures.

Establishing Emergency Communication Channels:

Use two-way radios, satellite phones, or CB radios to set up a communication network that functions independently of the grid. This network should have designated channels for emergency communication, ensuring that all homesteaders in the area can quickly alert each other during crises like fires, floods, or medical emergencies.

Create an emergency contact list that includes the names, locations, and communication methods for each homestead in the network. Distribute this list among community members to ensure that everyone knows whom to contact and how.

Cooperative Emergency Planning and Drills:

Organize community-wide emergency drills to practice responses to common threats such as wildfires, storms, or medical emergencies. Drills help identify potential weaknesses in the network and ensure that everyone is prepared to act swiftly.

Develop a community emergency plan that outlines the roles and responsibilities of each homestead in different scenarios. This might include designating individuals as medical responders, communications coordinators, or transportation providers.

Shared Resources and Cooperative Storage:

Establish community storage sites for emergency supplies such as food, water, medical kits, and backup power equipment. These shared caches provide a safety net for those whose supplies run low or are affected by disasters.

Collaborate on bulk purchases of critical items like seeds, fuel, and building materials, reducing costs for everyone involved. Establishing a cooperative purchasing system ensures that homesteaders have access to essential supplies at a lower cost.

Pooling Labor and Skills for Large Projects:

For large-scale tasks like barn raising, fencing, or harvests, organize cooperative workdays where multiple homesteads contribute labor and tools. These events build camaraderie and help complete projects faster and more efficiently than working alone.

Set up a time-banking system where homesteaders can trade labor hours. For example, helping one homestead build a fence could earn hours that can later be exchanged for help in your own garden or greenhouse construction.

Establishing Trust and Fairness in Trading and Bartering

Trust and fairness are the foundation of successful trading and bartering systems. Setting up fair trade practices and maintaining transparency ensures long-lasting, positive relationships within the community.

Creating Clear Trading Guidelines:

Develop a code of ethics for trading that emphasizes honesty, fair valuation, and mutual respect. Ensure that all trades are agreed upon with a clear understanding of what each party is offering and expecting in return.

Use trade logs to document bartering agreements, especially for more complex trades involving services like tool repairs or large-scale projects. This record helps maintain transparency and avoids misunderstandings.

Setting Up a Fair Valuation System:

Agree on a standard valuation system within your network to ensure that goods and services are traded fairly. This could involve setting basic equivalencies, such as one hour of labor for a dozen eggs, or establishing a point system for more complex trades.

Regularly revisit and adjust the valuation system to reflect seasonal availability, changes in resources, and feedback from community members.

Conflict Resolution Strategies:

In the event of disputes, establish a mediation process where neutral community members can help resolve disagreements. This process should focus on maintaining harmony and finding fair solutions that satisfy both parties.

Encourage a feedback loop where traders can provide constructive feedback on bartering interactions. This ensures continuous improvement in trade practices and builds trust within the network.

Building Cooperative Systems for Long-Term Community Support

Beyond emergency preparedness, developing cooperative systems that support long-term goals strengthens the homestead community and increases overall resilience.

Seed Banks and Shared Agricultural Resources:

Establish a community seed bank where homesteaders can contribute and withdraw seeds. This ensures a diverse and resilient crop base, allowing homesteads to adapt to changing conditions and reduce dependency on commercial seeds.

Coordinate the planting of different crops among homesteads to promote crop diversity and minimize competition. Sharing resources like compost or specialized gardening tools strengthens agricultural productivity across the network.

Collaborative Education and Skill-Building Programs:

Set up community workshops that rotate between homesteads, covering essential skills such as permaculture techniques, animal husbandry, and off-grid technology maintenance. These workshops provide opportunities for continuous learning and skill diversification.

Develop a mentorship program where experienced homesteaders partner with newcomers, guiding them through their first years of off-grid living. Mentorship builds strong relationships and ensures knowledge is passed down effectively.

Creating and Supporting Cooperative Businesses:

Support the development of cooperative businesses within the community, such as a shared dairy operation, blacksmith shop, or craft market. These businesses generate income and provide essential goods or services, benefiting everyone involved.

Use community investment methods, like pooling resources or offering labor in exchange for shares, to launch new projects that have mutual benefits. These could include building a communal processing facility for preserved foods or establishing a shared greenhouse for year-round produce.

Sustainable Water Management Systems:

Collaborate on building shared rainwater harvesting systems, reservoirs, or irrigation channels that serve multiple homesteads. These shared water systems are especially valuable during droughts or in areas with limited water access.

Establish a community water monitoring system to track usage and ensure that everyone has access to adequate supplies. This monitoring also helps identify potential contamination issues early, protecting the health and well-being of the entire network.

Renewable Energy and Shared Power Systems:

Set up shared renewable energy projects, like a cooperative wind turbine or solar farm, that provide power to multiple homesteads. This provides a more stable and cost-effective energy solution for the community, reducing individual reliance on expensive systems. By pooling resources, homesteaders can afford larger, more efficient setups that generate power for all participants.

Power Storage and Distribution: Develop a centralized battery bank or energy storage system where excess energy produced by shared solar panels or wind turbines can be stored and distributed as needed. This ensures power availability during periods of low production (e.g., cloudy days or low-wind conditions). Set up a fair distribution plan so that all participants have equal access to the stored power based on their energy needs.

Microgrid Development: For communities with multiple homesteads, consider building a microgrid, a localized energy grid that can operate independently from the main electrical grid.

Microgrids allow homesteads to share energy produced from various sources, such as solar, wind, or hydro, while maintaining the autonomy of each individual power system. If one system underperforms, the others can supplement it, ensuring uninterrupted power across the network.

Creating Social and Emotional Support Networks

In addition to material resources, emotional and social support is vital for maintaining a healthy and thriving off-grid community. Isolation can be a challenge for many homesteaders, and fostering a sense of community can help mitigate feelings of loneliness while reinforcing a culture of mutual aid.

Regular Community Gatherings and Social Events:

Organize regular community meals, celebrations, or workshop days where homesteaders can come together, share food, and socialize. These events help build strong relationships and provide a break from the daily routine of homesteading, encouraging relaxation and camaraderie.

Seasonal festivals or harvest celebrations can also be significant community-building events. Sharing the bounty of each homestead strengthens the bonds between members and reinforces a sense of shared success and cooperation.

Emotional Support Systems:

Create an informal system of emotional check-ins where homesteaders regularly visit or call each other to provide encouragement and mental support. These small acts of care can make a big difference, especially during challenging seasons or times of personal struggle.

Offer peer counseling or community talking circles where members can openly discuss the challenges of off-grid living, share coping strategies, and offer each other advice. These support systems help reduce the mental strain that can arise from the unique demands of an off-grid lifestyle.

Mentorship and Knowledge Sharing:

Encourage experienced homesteaders to mentor newcomers to the community. Mentorship provides practical advice and reassurance, helping newcomers adapt to the challenges of off-grid living and creating a cycle of knowledge sharing that benefits the entire community.

Establish a knowledge library where homesteaders can contribute books, manuals, and other educational resources on topics like permaculture, renewable energy systems, or animal care. This collective resource is a valuable asset for both current and future generations of homesteaders.

Building Conflict Resolution Mechanisms:

Conflict is inevitable in any community, but having clear, respectful conflict resolution strategies in place is key to maintaining harmony. Establish a community mediation process where neutral parties help resolve disputes amicably and fairly.

Create guidelines for respectful communication that all members agree to follow. This ensures that disagreements are addressed constructively and that every voice is heard without escalating tensions.

Collaborative Planning for Future Community Growth

As the community grows, planning for long-term sustainability and development becomes critical. By working together to anticipate future needs and opportunities, homesteaders can ensure that the community continues to thrive.

Long-Term Infrastructure Planning:

Plan for the expansion of shared infrastructure such as water systems, roads, and communication networks to accommodate new members or future growth. Ensure that new projects are integrated into the overall community vision, promoting sustainability and ease of access.

Encourage community land stewardship by setting aside communal spaces for shared use, such as community gardens, orchards, or pasture land. This helps avoid overuse of individual resources while promoting cooperative management of the land.

Developing Community Leadership and Governance:

Establish a community council or leadership group that can organize and oversee larger projects, facilitate decision-making, and represent the interests of all community members. Rotating leadership roles can help ensure that everyone has a say in the direction of the community.

Develop a community charter or agreement that outlines the shared values, principles, and goals of the homestead network. This document can help guide decisions, maintain a sense of unity, and resolve potential disputes by clearly defining expectations for all members.

Economic Development and Sustainability:

Support community members in developing cottage industries that generate income for the homestead network. This could include selling handmade goods, preserves, livestock products, or renewable energy to nearby towns or through cooperative markets. By creating diverse revenue streams, the community can build financial resilience.

Encourage investment in sustainable technology and eco-friendly practices to further reduce dependency on outside resources. This includes promoting permaculture farming techniques, expanding renewable energy systems, and implementing zero-waste principles across all homesteads.

Adapting to Environmental and Social Changes:

As environmental conditions shift, the community should continuously assess and adapt its practices to ensure resilience. This might involve switching crops to more drought-tolerant varieties, enhancing water conservation measures, or rethinking land-use strategies to accommodate climate changes.

Remain open to the growth and evolution of the community, welcoming new ideas and members who bring fresh perspectives. By staying adaptable and forward-thinking, the community can continue to thrive in a changing world.

Conclusion: Strengthening Community Through Cooperation and Shared Values

Bartering, trading, and building a community are essential elements of off-grid living that provide a wealth of resources, knowledge, and support. By fostering strong relationships with fellow homesteaders, practicing fairness and trust in trading, and developing collaborative systems for mutual aid, you create a resilient and interconnected community. This network not only enhances your self-sufficiency but also ensures a safety net in times of crisis, promoting long-term sustainability and collective well-being.

In the next chapter, we will explore preserving and processing food for long-term storage, focusing on canning, drying, fermenting, and other methods to ensure your homestead remains well-stocked throughout the year.

Chapter 24: Preparing for Long-Term Success

Off-grid living is not a static lifestyle; it requires continual adaptation, planning, and evaluation to ensure that you maintain sustainability and growth over the long term. Setting goals, keeping detailed records, and reviewing your practices regularly allow you to track progress, manage resources efficiently, and make informed decisions that enhance your homestead's resilience and productivity. This chapter focuses on strategies for setting achievable goals, tracking production and energy use, and reviewing and adapting your off-grid lifestyle for maximum efficiency and sustainability.

Setting Goals for Continued Growth and Sustainability

Establishing clear and achievable goals is essential for the long-term success of an off-grid homestead. These goals should focus on both immediate needs and future development to ensure that your homestead continues to grow and thrive.

Short-Term Goals (1-2 Years):

Infrastructure and Energy Improvements: Set specific goals for upgrading or expanding your energy systems, such as installing additional solar panels, improving wind turbine efficiency, or expanding your battery storage capacity. These upgrades ensure a more stable and sufficient energy supply, allowing you to support additional structures or appliances in the future.

Food Production Expansion: Focus on increasing the productivity of your garden or orchard by adding new crops, installing an irrigation system, or expanding greenhouse space. Consider diversifying your livestock to include additional protein sources like goats for milk or ducks for eggs.

Water Management Upgrades: Implement goals to improve water conservation and storage, such as building new rainwater catchment systems, digging additional wells, or upgrading filtration systems. Efficient water management is crucial for maintaining crop yields and supporting livestock, particularly in drier regions.

Medium-Term Goals (3-5 Years):

Building and Expanding Outbuildings: Plan to build or expand essential structures like barns, coops, or tool sheds. These expansions support a larger scale of operations and provide spaces for storage, animal care, or equipment maintenance. For example, building a larger barn may enable you to raise additional livestock or store more feed, increasing overall food security.

Increasing Crop Diversity and Yield: Focus on establishing perennial gardens, fruit orchards, and herb gardens that provide long-term, sustainable yields. Implement crop rotation and permaculture practices to improve soil health and reduce pest infestations, ensuring the productivity of your land.

Renewable Energy System Optimization: As your homestead grows, set goals for enhancing energy efficiency by upgrading to high-efficiency inverters, expanding solar arrays, or integrating new technologies like hydro systems if you have access to water sources. These upgrades ensure that your homestead remains energy self-sufficient as you add new systems or appliances.

Long-Term Goals (5+ Years):

Achieving Food Independence: Set goals for complete food self-sufficiency by ensuring that your homestead produces all the food you need year-round. This includes expanding gardens, orchards, livestock, and developing efficient preservation methods like canning, fermenting, and drying to store surplus food for winter months.

Building Community Ties: Focus on integrating with local homesteader networks and forming long-term cooperative partnerships. Goals could include establishing a barter market or creating shared resources such as community seed banks or tool libraries, which reduce costs and enhance the resilience of your homestead.

Developing a Legacy Plan: Consider the future of your homestead by setting goals that prepare it for the next generation. This might involve planting long-term crops, such as nut trees, that will yield in future decades, or creating a knowledge repository that documents homesteading practices, ensuring continuity and sustainability for those who follow.

Keeping Records of Production, Energy Use, and Progress

Accurate and consistent record-keeping is essential for understanding the efficiency and output of your homestead. By documenting production levels, energy usage, and other key metrics, you can identify areas for improvement and make informed decisions about future upgrades and resource management.

Documenting Crop Yields and Garden Productivity:

Planting and Harvesting Logs: Keep detailed records of what you plant, when you plant it, and the yield you harvest. Note any issues encountered, such as pests or diseases, and the solutions you implemented. This helps you understand which crops perform best under specific conditions and refine your planting schedule each year.

Soil Health Monitoring: Regularly test soil pH, nutrient levels, and organic matter content. Maintain a soil health log to track improvements over time as you implement new composting or fertilization methods. Documenting these details helps you adapt your soil management practices for increased productivity.

Tracking Livestock Production and Care:

Animal Health Records: Keep detailed logs of your animals' health, including vaccinations, breeding schedules, milk or egg production, and any medical treatments administered. This information is critical for managing livestock efficiently and ensuring their well-being.

Feed and Output Ratios: Document how much feed your animals consume compared to the outputs they provide (e.g., milk, eggs, meat). This helps you optimize feeding schedules and improve the efficiency of your livestock management practices over time.

Energy Use and Renewable System Monitoring:

Solar, Wind, and Hydro Logs: Track the daily and seasonal output of your energy systems. Monitor solar panel performance, wind turbine activity, and hydro generator output to identify patterns and fluctuations. Understanding these patterns helps you adjust your energy use, schedule maintenance, and make necessary system adjustments.

Battery and Inverter Monitoring: Maintain records of battery charge levels, cycles, and performance metrics. This information is vital for managing battery life and ensuring that your energy storage systems are functioning properly. Note any discrepancies or declines in performance to address them promptly before they impact your power availability.

Maintaining a Homestead Journal:

A homestead journal is a valuable tool for tracking the progress of various projects and the overall development of your off-grid lifestyle. Document successes, failures, and adaptations made in response to challenges. This continuous record helps identify trends and inform future planning.

Include sections for weather patterns, seasonal observations, and any experimental projects you undertake, such as testing new crop varieties or alternative building techniques. This information provides a long-term perspective that enhances your ability to anticipate and prepare for future needs.

Reviewing and Adapting Your Off-Grid Lifestyle for Greater Efficiency

To achieve long-term sustainability, it's essential to periodically review your lifestyle, evaluate what is working, and make adaptations where necessary. Regular assessments allow you to stay ahead of potential problems and continually improve your homestead's efficiency.

Annual Review of Homestead Performance:

Production Analysis: At the end of each growing season, review your crop yields and compare them to previous years. Analyze which crops performed best and why, and adjust your planting strategy for the next season based on these observations. Consider factors like soil conditions, watering schedules, and pest control methods.

Livestock Review: Assess the productivity and health of your livestock over the year. Determine whether adjustments to feeding routines, housing, or veterinary care are needed. If certain animals are not producing as expected, decide whether to cull, replace, or diversify your livestock options.

Energy Efficiency Evaluation: Review the efficiency of your energy systems by analyzing power production data and energy consumption records. Identify times when energy output was insufficient and consider whether upgrades or additional renewable systems are needed to balance supply and demand.

Seasonal Adaptation Strategies:

Adapting for Weather Variability: Depending on your location, seasonal weather patterns may vary significantly. Prepare for changes by adjusting planting schedules, building seasonal animal shelters, or enhancing insulation in outbuildings. Installing windbreaks or shading systems can also help manage extreme weather conditions like heatwaves or strong winds.

Winterization and Summer Prep: At the start of each winter or summer, prepare your homestead for the coming season. This might involve insulating greenhouses, storing water reserves, or setting up cooling systems for animal shelters. Document the steps taken each season and their effectiveness to refine your approach year after year.

Efficiency Improvements and Technology Upgrades:

Evaluating Tool and Equipment Efficiency: Assess whether your tools and equipment are meeting your needs. Consider upgrading to more efficient or durable models if existing equipment is underperforming or needs frequent repairs. Investing in high-quality tools can reduce labor and improve productivity.

Renewable System Upgrades: If your homestead has grown since you initially installed energy systems, evaluate whether your current setup can handle the increased load. Consider adding more solar panels, upgrading wind turbines, or integrating hybrid systems that combine multiple energy sources to maximize efficiency.

Financial Planning and Resource Allocation:

Budget Review: Review your budget and expenses annually, tracking costs associated with energy systems, animal feed, seeds, and maintenance. Determine which areas offer potential for cost reduction, such as producing your own animal feed or investing in bulk seed purchases. Allocate resources towards projects that promise long-term savings or increased production capacity.

Emergency Fund and Contingency Planning: Ensure that you maintain an emergency fund to cover unexpected expenses, such as repairs to critical systems or medical needs for livestock. Develop a contingency plan that outlines how you will respond to emergencies like natural disasters or prolonged equipment failures.

Long-Term Lifestyle Adaptations for Greater Sustainability

Adapting your lifestyle to increase efficiency and reduce reliance on external resources ensures long-term success. By continuously seeking ways to optimize your homestead, you build resilience and improve self-sufficiency.

Implementing Zero-Waste Principles:

Strive to reduce waste by reusing materials, composting organic matter, and recycling wherever possible. Implement a composting toilet system, or build a biogas digester that uses organic waste to produce cooking fuel. Minimizing waste not only benefits the environment but also reduces dependency on outside inputs.

Create closed-loop systems that recycle nutrients, water, and energy. For example, use greywater from showers and sinks to irrigate gardens, or integrate chicken coops with composting systems to fertilize soil naturally.

Expanding Food Preservation and Storage Capabilities:

As your homestead's food production increases, adapt by expanding preservation techniques. Experiment with canning, fermenting, freeze-drying, and root cellaring to extend the shelf life of fruits, vegetables, and meats. Properly stored, these preserved foods provide security during lean seasons and reduce waste from overabundance during harvest times.

Building Cold Storage Solutions: Constructing root cellars, installing solar-powered refrigerators, or building insulated storage spaces for winter use can significantly enhance your food storage capabilities. These adaptations help maintain a steady food supply throughout the year, ensuring that no surplus goes to waste.

Permaculture and Regenerative Agriculture Practices:

Incorporate permaculture principles like companion planting, polycultures, and no-till gardening to improve soil health and increase yields. These practices reduce labor and create ecosystems that support one another, enhancing the long-term productivity of your homestead.

Explore regenerative agriculture methods such as rotational grazing, which allows livestock to naturally fertilize and restore soil health while providing space for different plants to grow. These methods build resilience into your homestead, ensuring that your land remains fertile and productive over the decades.

Learning and Adapting Through Research and Community Involvement:

Stay informed about advancements in off-grid technologies, sustainable agriculture, and renewable energy solutions by attending workshops, reading research articles, and participating in local homesteader gatherings. Knowledge-sharing helps you adapt and incorporate new methods that enhance your homestead's efficiency.

Work closely with other homesteaders in your community to share insights, experiences, and resources. Cooperating with neighbors can reveal new strategies for managing challenges like water scarcity, soil degradation, or energy shortages, leading to mutually beneficial solutions.

Creating a Personal and Homestead Growth Log

To ensure continued progress and adaptation, keep a personal and homestead growth log that records not only physical developments but also the skills and knowledge you gain along the way. This log serves as both a practical tool and a personal journal that tracks your journey toward self-sufficiency.

Recording Achievements and Lessons Learned:

Document milestones such as successful harvests, new structures built, or energy system upgrades. Note the challenges faced and the solutions implemented, as this information can help you or others adapt similar strategies in the future.

Include reflections on personal growth, such as learning new skills like carpentry, herbal medicine preparation, or livestock management. These records provide a sense of accomplishment and encourage continuous learning.

Setting New Goals Based on Past Performance:

Use the data and reflections in your log to set new goals. For example, if you documented a particularly successful growing season, identify the practices that contributed to that success and set a goal to replicate or expand those practices.

Track annual improvements in efficiency, such as increased energy production or decreased water usage, and use these metrics to guide your long-term planning. Evaluating these trends helps you refine your lifestyle and align future goals with proven success.

Maintaining Adaptability and Flexibility:

Recognize that the off-grid lifestyle is dynamic and requires ongoing flexibility. Set goals that allow for adjustments based on environmental conditions, new technologies, or evolving personal needs. A flexible approach ensures that your homestead remains sustainable even as circumstances change.

Be open to scaling back certain operations if they prove inefficient or unsustainable. For example, if a particular crop requires too much water or labor, consider transitioning to a drought-resistant variety or planting something that better suits your climate and resources.

Conclusion: Building a Sustainable, Efficient Off-Grid Future

Preparing for long-term success in an off-grid lifestyle means setting clear goals, keeping accurate records, and continuously adapting practices to ensure greater efficiency and sustainability. By reviewing your progress and making informed decisions based on data and experience, you build a resilient homestead that grows stronger over time. With a focus on sustainable growth, energy efficiency, and community cooperation, your homestead can thrive for generations, supporting not only your immediate needs but also contributing to a larger network of self-sufficient communities.

In the next chapter, we will explore crafting and maintaining essential tools, focusing on building durable and effective tools for hunting, trapping, and daily use on the homestead.

Chapter 25: The Future of Off-Grid Living

Off-grid living continues to evolve, with advancements in technology, growing awareness of environmental impact, and a shift towards sustainable and ethical practices. As the off-grid lifestyle becomes increasingly popular, new tools and innovations are emerging that enhance efficiency, minimize ecological footprints, and provide more resilient ways to live independently. This chapter explores the evolving landscape of off-grid living, the ethical considerations homesteaders face, and provides final tips for maintaining a successful, sustainable lifestyle.

The Evolving Landscape of Sustainable Living and New Technologies

Modern off-grid living is no longer limited to traditional practices; it now integrates advanced technologies that improve efficiency and make sustainability more achievable. Understanding and incorporating these developments can significantly enhance your homestead's productivity and resilience.

Emerging Renewable Energy Technologies:

High-Efficiency Solar Panels: Advances in solar panel technology, such as bifacial panels and thin-film modules, allow for greater energy capture and efficiency, even in low-light conditions. These new panels are lightweight, flexible, and can be integrated into unconventional spaces, such as roofs with non-ideal angles or walls.

Hydrogen Fuel Cells: Hydrogen fuel cells are gaining traction as a backup or supplemental power source. These cells convert hydrogen into electricity with only water as a byproduct, making them a clean and efficient option for off-grid power storage.

Wind Turbines with Vertical Axis Technology: Vertical axis wind turbines (VAWTs) are designed to operate in areas with variable wind patterns. These compact turbines are less intrusive, quieter, and can generate power even when wind direction fluctuates, making them suitable for smaller homesteads.

Water Conservation and Purification Innovations:

Atmospheric Water Generators: These devices extract water from the air using condensation, providing an additional source of fresh water in humid regions. Paired with solar or wind power, these systems offer a sustainable way to increase water self-sufficiency without relying on traditional sources like rainwater or wells.

Greywater Recycling Systems: Greywater systems are becoming more advanced, with modular designs that filter and reuse water from showers, sinks, and washing machines for garden irrigation. Newer models are equipped with smart controls that optimize water use based on soil moisture levels, ensuring that plants receive the right amount of water without waste.

Ultraviolet (UV) and Ozone Water Purification: UV and ozone purification systems provide chemical-free water treatment, killing bacteria and pathogens efficiently. These systems are ideal for homesteads with access to surface water sources that require ongoing purification for safe use.

Smart Technology for Off-Grid Management:

Home Energy Management Systems (HEMS): HEMS technology allows homesteaders to monitor and control energy usage in real-time. These systems provide data on energy production from solar, wind, or hydro systems and allow for remote control of appliances, optimizing energy efficiency even when you're not on-site.

Smart Irrigation Systems: Integrated with weather data and soil moisture sensors, smart irrigation systems automatically adjust watering schedules based on real-time conditions. These systems reduce water use and ensure that crops receive adequate hydration, particularly during dry periods.

Automated Livestock Monitoring: GPS collars and smart sensors can track livestock health and movement, sending alerts for unusual behavior that may indicate illness or predation. These technologies help homesteaders manage animals more efficiently, especially when livestock are grazing over large areas.

Sustainable Building Materials and Techniques:

Hempcrete and Sustainable Insulation: Hempcrete, a building material made from hemp, lime, and water, is becoming popular for its high insulation properties and sustainability. This material is non-toxic, mold-resistant, and has a low carbon footprint, making it an ideal choice for off-grid structures.

3D-Printed Homes: Using natural materials like clay or recycled concrete, 3D-printed homes are revolutionizing the construction of off-grid shelters. These homes are quick to build, customizable, and can be designed with energy-efficient features like passive solar heating and natural ventilation systems.

Solar Roof Tiles: Integrating solar panels directly into roofing materials, solar roof tiles provide a dual function—generating energy while protecting your home. These tiles are particularly beneficial for those looking to minimize visual impact while maximizing energy production.

Environmental Impact and Ethical Considerations for Homesteaders

As more people adopt off-grid lifestyles, it is essential to consider the broader impact on the environment and the ethical implications of homesteading practices. Making informed, responsible decisions ensures that your lifestyle remains sustainable and beneficial to both the local ecosystem and the wider environment.

Land Management and Wildlife Preservation:

Sustainable Land Use: Homesteaders must be mindful of their impact on the land, ensuring that clearing, planting, and building activities do not disrupt local wildlife habitats. Implementing no-till gardening, rotational grazing, and agroforestry practices helps maintain soil health and biodiversity while providing for your needs.

Coexisting with Wildlife: Ethical homesteading involves coexisting with native species rather than displacing them. Fencing systems designed to keep out large predators, like bears, should still allow for the free movement of smaller animals. Using non-lethal deterrents and creating buffer zones around sensitive areas, such as nesting sites or migration paths, supports wildlife conservation.

Water Rights and Resource Sharing:

Respecting Water Rights: In areas where water resources are shared, such as rivers or aquifers, homesteaders must be aware of local regulations and agreements regarding water use. Over-extraction can affect neighboring communities and ecosystems, so it's essential to use water conservatively and implement rainwater harvesting or greywater systems to supplement natural sources.

Supporting Community Resources: Homesteaders can contribute positively by sharing water resources, such as allowing neighbors to access wells during droughts or cooperating in the construction of communal water systems. This practice promotes community solidarity and reduces competition for limited resources.

Avoiding Over-Exploitation of Natural Resources:

Sustainable Forestry Practices: When using wood for fuel or building, ensure that you harvest sustainably by implementing selective logging and replanting strategies. Overharvesting can lead to deforestation, soil erosion, and loss of biodiversity, so aim to maintain a balance that supports forest regeneration.

Ethical Hunting and Fishing: If your homestead relies on hunting or fishing for protein, practice ethical methods by following local regulations, respecting hunting seasons, and only taking what is necessary. Avoid overfishing or hunting species that are threatened or have declining populations.

Minimizing Carbon Footprint and Waste:

Renewable Energy Optimization: Maximize the efficiency of renewable systems to minimize your homestead's carbon footprint. Using excess power for heating, water pumping, or charging batteries ensures that no energy goes to waste. Employing biofuel systems or biomass heaters that use organic waste further reduces reliance on fossil fuels.

Zero-Waste Practices: Aim to reduce, reuse, and recycle wherever possible. Compost organic waste, repurpose building materials, and minimize packaging by buying in bulk or growing your own supplies. Implementing a zero-waste mindset helps preserve resources and minimizes the environmental impact of off-grid living.

Final Tips for Maintaining a Successful Off-Grid Lifestyle

Prioritize Flexibility and Adaptability:

The success of an off-grid homestead depends on your ability to adapt to changing conditions, whether it's a shift in weather patterns, new technology, or personal needs. Maintain flexibility in your systems and lifestyle so you can adjust quickly and effectively.

Regularly review your goals, energy usage, food production, and water management strategies to identify areas for improvement. Keeping an open mind and being willing to experiment with new ideas ensures that your homestead remains resilient.

Continuously Invest in Knowledge and Skills:

Off-grid living requires a diverse skill set, from carpentry and gardening to first aid and animal care. Dedicate time to learning new skills and staying updated on innovations in sustainable living. Consider online courses, workshops, and community gatherings as opportunities for growth.

Document your learning experiences in a homestead journal, noting what worked, what didn't, and why. This record serves as a valuable resource for continuous improvement and future planning.

Build a Reliable Support Network:

Success in off-grid living often depends on having a strong network of like-minded individuals. Engage with local communities, online forums, or homesteading networks to exchange ideas, trade resources, and provide mutual support.

Establish partnerships with neighbors for collaborative projects like shared gardens, livestock exchanges, or energy co-ops. These networks create resilience, ensuring that when challenges arise, you have the support needed to overcome them.

Focus on Long-Term Sustainability:

Design systems with long-term sustainability in mind. Invest in quality materials for buildings and infrastructure, implement renewable energy systems that are scalable, and focus on growing perennial crops that produce food year after year with minimal input.

Monitor and assess the environmental impact of your homestead regularly. Make adjustments as necessary to minimize harm, whether it involves rotating crops, planting trees for carbon sequestration, or expanding rainwater catchment systems.

Practice Self-Sufficiency Without Isolation:

While independence is a core value of off-grid living, it doesn't mean you need to live in isolation. Cultivate a balance between self-sufficiency and community interaction. Trading, sharing knowledge, and cooperating with others enriches your experience and contributes to a broader culture of sustainability.

Use the skills and resources you gain to educate and support others interested in off-grid living. Sharing knowledge strengthens community bonds and promotes a more widespread adoption of sustainable practices, creating a network of homesteads that collectively build a resilient future.

Looking Ahead: The Future of Off-Grid Living

Integrating Off-Grid Communities with Sustainable Development Goals:

As awareness of environmental issues grows, off-grid communities are increasingly viewed as models for sustainable development. By integrating best practices in agriculture, energy production, and waste management, these communities can demonstrate effective solutions to larger societal challenges like food security, energy independence, and ecological preservation.

Homesteaders who actively engage with policy makers and environmental organizations can contribute their expertise, helping to shape regulations and programs that support sustainable, off-grid lifestyles. This advocacy also ensures that off-grid living remains a viable option for more people in the future.

Embracing Technological and Social Innovations:

The future of off-grid living will likely be shaped by continued advancements in technology and shifting social attitudes toward sustainability. Staying open to new innovations, such as eco-friendly building materials, off-grid internet solutions, and autonomous gardening systems, keeps your homestead efficient and adaptable.

Participate in local and global movements that promote sustainable and ethical practices. Supporting initiatives like community land trusts or permaculture design courses expands the reach and impact of the off-grid movement, creating opportunities for collaboration and shared progress.

Final Reflections

Off-grid living is a rewarding but complex lifestyle that requires careful planning, ongoing adaptation, and a commitment to sustainability. By focusing on flexibility, continual learning, and building strong community ties, homesteaders can create thriving, resilient environments that not only support their own needs but also contribute positively to the broader ecosystem.

In a rapidly changing world, off-grid living stands as a testament to the power of self-sufficiency, ecological stewardship, and sustainable development. Whether through technological innovations, ethical practices, or cooperative community efforts, those who choose this path have the opportunity to live in harmony with nature while paving the way for future generations to do the same.

Conclusion: A Sustainable Path Forward

This book has explored the comprehensive steps, strategies, and practices necessary for establishing and maintaining an off-grid homestead. From the basics of energy systems, gardening, and livestock management to the nuances of building community ties and integrating new technologies, the knowledge shared aims to equip aspiring and experienced homesteaders alike.

As you continue your off-grid journey, remember that success is not measured by independence alone but by your ability to live sustainably, adapt effectively, and engage with others in a spirit of cooperation and shared growth. The future of off-grid living is bright, and with each step, you contribute to a movement that seeks to balance human needs with the preservation and enhancement of the natural world.

Made in the USA
Monee, IL
21 November 2024

70788550R00103